AHA! Workshop on Information Discovery in Text 2014

Held at COLING 2014

Dublin, Ireland
23 August 2014

ISBN: 978-1-63439-215-0

Printed from e-media with permission by:

Curran Associates, Inc.
57 Morehouse Lane
Red Hook, NY 12571

Some format issues inherent in the e-media version may also appear in this print version.

Printed by Curran Associates, Inc. (2014)

For permission requests, please contact the Association for Computational Linguistics at the address below.

Association for Computational Linguistics
209 N. Eighth Street
Stroudsburg, Pennsylvania 18360

Phone: 1-570-476-8006
Fax: 1-570-476-0860

acl@aclweb.org

Additional copies of this publication are available from:

Curran Associates, Inc.
57 Morehouse Lane
Red Hook, NY 12571 USA
Phone: 845-758-0400
Fax: 845-758-2634
Email: curran@proceedings.com
Web: www.proceedings.com

Introduction

Welcome to the First AHA!-Workshop on Information Discovery in Text!

In this workshop, we are bringing together leading researchers in the emerging field of Information Discovery to discuss approaches for Information Extraction that are not bound by a pre-specified schema of information, but rather discover relational or categorial structure automatically from given unstructured data.

This includes approaches that are based on unsupervised machine-learning over models of distributional semantics, as well as OpenIE methods that relax the definition of semantic relations in order to more openly extract structured information. Other approaches focus on inexpensively training information extractors to be used across different domains with minimal supervision, or on adapting existing IE systems to new domains and relations.

As different approaches on Information Discovery are gaining momentum, many fundamental questions arise that merit discussion: How do these approaches compare and what are their relative strengths and weaknesses? What are the desiderata and applications for Information Discovery methods? How can such methods be evaluated and compared? And most importantly, what is the potential of Information Discovery methods and where can current research lead?

We received 19 paper submissions of which the programme committee has accepted ten - six of which were chosen for oral presentation and four as posters.

We look forward to a workshop full of interesting paper presentations, invited talks and lively discussion.

Sincerely,

Alan Akbik and Larysa Visengeriyeva

AHA! Chairs

Workshop Chairs and Organizers

Alan Akbik, Technische Universität Berlin

Larysa Visengeriyeva, Technische Universität Berlin

Programme Committee

Isabelle Augenstein, University of Sheffield

Christoph Boden, Technische Universität Berlin

Danushka Bollegala, University of Liverpool

Leon Derczynski, University of Sheffield

Jonathan Gordon, University of Rochester

Max Heimel, Technische Universität Berlin

Holmer Hemsen, Technische Universität Berlin

Johannes Kirschnick, Technische Universität Berlin

Xiao Ling, University of Washington

Steffen Remus, Technische Universität Darmstadt

Martin Riedl, Technische Universität Darmstadt

Tim Rocktäschel, University College London

Vivek Srikumar, Stanford University

Mark Steedman, University of Edinburgh

Andreas Vlachos, University College London

Gerhard Weikum, Max Plank Institute Saarbrücken

Limin Yao, University of Massachusetts

Steering Committee

Hans Uszkoreit, German Center for Artificial Intelligence

Volker Markl, Technische Universität Berlin

Table of Contents

Conference Program

Application-Driven Relation Extraction with Limited Distant Supervision

Andreas Vlachos
Computer Science Department
University College London
a.vlachos@cs.ucl.ac.uk

Stephen Clark
Computer Laboratory
University of Cambridge
sc609@cam.ac.uk

Abstract

Recent approaches to relation extraction following the distant supervision paradigm have focused on exploiting large knowledge bases, from which they extract substantial amount of supervision. However, for many relations in real-world applications, there are few instances available to seed the relation extraction process, and appropriate named entity recognizers which are necessary for pre-processing do not exist. To overcome this issue, we learn entity filters jointly with relation extraction using imitation learning. We evaluate our approach on architect names and building completion years, using only around 30 seed instances for each relation and show that the jointly learned entity filters improved the performance by 30 and 7 points in average precision.

1 Introduction

In this paper we focus on relation extraction in the context of a real-world application. The application is a dialog-based city tour guide, based in Edinburgh. One of the features of the system is its pro-active nature, offering information which may be of interest to the user. In order to be pro-active in this way, as well as answer users' questions, the system requires a large amount of knowledge about the city. Part of that knowledge is stored in a database, which is time-consuming and difficult to populate manually. Hence, we have explored the use of an automatic knowledge base population technique based on distant supervision (Craven and Kumlien, 1999; Mintz et al., 2009).

The attraction of this approach is that the only input required is a list of seed instances of the relation in question and a corpus of sentences expressing new instances of that relation. However, existing studies typically assume a large seed set, whereas in our application such sets are often not readily available, e.g. Mintz et al. (2009) reported using 7K-140K seed instances per relation as input. In this paper, the two relations that we evaluate on are architect name and completion year of buildings. These were chosen because they are highly relevant to our application, but also somewhat non-standard compared to the existing literature; and crucially they do not come with a readily-available set of seed instances.

Furthermore, previous approaches typically assume named entity recognition (NER) as a pre-processing step in order to construct the training and testing instances. However, since these tools are not tailored to the relations of interest, they introduce spurious entity matches that are harmful to performance as shown by Ling and Weld (2012) and Zhang et al. (2013). These authors ameliorated this issue by learning fine-grained entity recognizers and filters using supervised learning. The labeled data used was extracted from the anchor text of entity mentions annotated in Wikipedia, however this is not possible for entities not annotated in this resource.

In this work, instead of relying on labeled data to construct entity filters, we learn them jointly with the relation extraction component. For this purpose we use the imitation learning algorithm DAGGER (Ross et al., 2011), which can handle the dependencies between actions taken in a sequence, and use supervision for later actions to learn how to take actions earlier in the sequence. We evaluate our approach using around 30 seed instances per relation and show that the jointly learned entity filters result in gains of 7 and 30 points in average precision for the completion year and the architect name relations respectively.

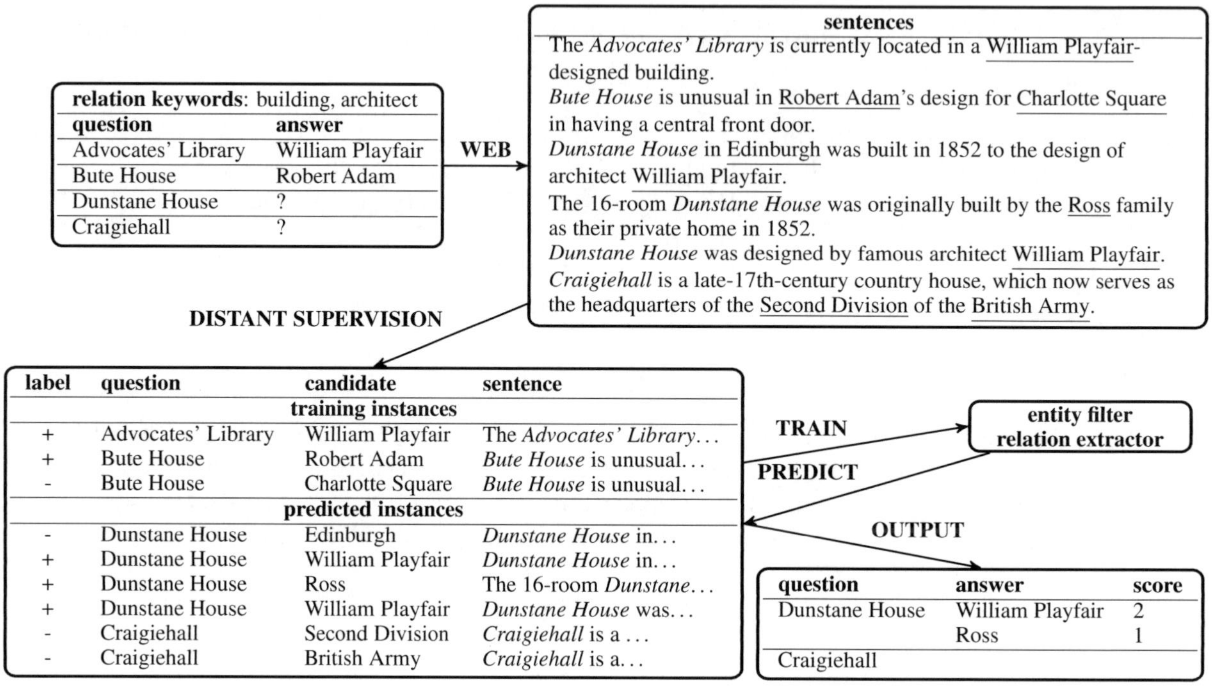

Figure 1: The stages of our proposed approach applied to the architect name relation.

2 Approach overview

We will use the architect-building relation as an example to give an overview of our approach, as shown in Figure 1. The input to the system is a list of buildings, where for some we know the architect (the seeds), and the task is to find the architects for the remainder. One difference with the standard setup for relation extraction using distant supervision is that we assume a list of historical buildings instead of a tailored NER system. This is reasonable for the example, since such a list is relatively easy to acquire. In order to create training data, queries containing words from the seeds are sent to a search engine. Sentences from the returned pages are then processed to find examples which contain mentions of both a building and the corresponding architect. Applying the distant supervision hypothesis, we assume that such sentences are indeed expressing the desired relation, and these are positive examples. While such data contains noise, it has been shown to be useful in practice (Yao et al., 2010; Hoffmann et al., 2011).

At test time the input is the name of a historical building. Now the web is searched to find example sentences containing this name, and the classifier is applied to each sentence, returning either the name of the architect, or none. Note that different sentences could provide evidence for different architects; hence assuming only one architect for each building, a procedure is required to decide between the possible answers (see Sec. 5).

3 Entity Filtering for Relation Extraction

Each relation extraction instance consists of a sentence containing a question entity (e.g. *Bute House*) and a candidate answer (e.g. *Robert Adam*), and the task is to predict whether the answer and question entity have the relation of interest. The standard approach is to learn a binary classifier (possibly as part of a more complex model e.g. Hoffmann et al. (2011)) using features that describe each entity as well as the lexico-syntactic relation between them in the sentence. These commonly include the lexicalized dependency path from the question entity to the candidate answer, as well as the lemmas on this path. In this setup, NER assists by filtering the instances generated to those that contain appropriate recognized entities and by providing features for them.

However, since we do not assume NER in pre-processing, this task becomes harder in our setup, since the candidate answers are very often inappropriate for the relation at question. A simple way

Algorithm 1: Learning with DAGGER

Input: training set $\mathcal{S}$, loss ℓ, CSC learner *CSCL*
Output: Learned policy H_N

1 CSC Examples $E = \emptyset$
2 **for** $i = 1$ **to** N **do**
3   **for** s ***in*** S **do**
4   Predict $\hat{y}_{1:T} = H_{i-1}(s)$
5   **for** $\hat{y}_t$ ***in*** $\pi(s)$ **do**
6   Extract features $\Phi_t = f(s, \hat{y}_{1:t-1})$
7   **foreach** *possible action* y_t^j **do**
8   Predict $y'_{t+1:T} = H_{i-1}(s; \hat{y}_{1:t-1}, y_t^j)$
9   Assess $c_t^j = \ell(\hat{y}_{1:t-1}, y_t^j, y'_{t+1:T})$
10   Add (Φ_t, c_t) to E
11   Learn $H_i = CSCL(E)$

to incorporate NER-like information is to add the features that would have been used for NER to the relation extraction features and learn a classifier as above. Such features are commonly extracted from the candidate answer itself as well as its context. The former include the tokens of the answer, their lemmas, whether the answer is capitalised, etc. The latter include the words and bigrams preceding and following the answer, as well as syntactic dependencies between the words denoting the entity and surrounding lemmas.

However, while these features are likely to be useful, they also render learning relation extraction harder because they are not directly relevant to the task. For example, the features describing the first training instance of Fig. 1 would include that the token *Playfair* is part of the candidate answer and that the lemma *design* is part on the syntactic dependency path between the architect and the building, but only the latter is crucial for the correct classification of this instance. Thus, including the NER features about the candidate answer can be misleading, especially since they tend to be less sparse than the relation extraction ones.

Therefore we split the prediction into two binary classification stages: the first stage predicts whether the candidate answer is appropriate for the relation (entity filtering), and the second one whether the sentence expresses the relation between the answer and the question entity (relation extraction). If the prediction for the first stage is negative, then the second stage is not reached. However, we do not have labels to train a classifier for the entity filtering stage since if an instance is negative this could be either due to the candidate answer or to the relation expressed in the sentence. We discuss how we overcome this issue using the algorithm DAGGER (Ross et al., 2011) next.

4 Imitation learning with DAGGER

Imitation learning algorithms such as DAGGER and SEARN (Daumé III et al., 2009) have been applied successfully to a variety of structured prediction tasks (Vlachos, 2012; He et al., 2013) due to their flexibility in incorporating features. In this work we focus on the parameter-free version of DAGGER and highlight its ability to handle missing labels in the training data. During training, DAGGER converts the problem of learning how to predict sequences of actions into cost sensitive classification (CSC) learning. The dependencies between the actions are learned by appropriate generation of CSC examples. In our case, each instance is predicted by a sequence of two actions: an entity filtering action followed (if positive) by a relation extraction action. The output is a learned policy, consisting of the binary classifiers for entity filtering and relation extraction.

Following Alg. 1, in each iteration DAGGER generates training examples using the previous learned policy H_{i-1} to predict the instances (line 4). For each action taken, the cost for each possible action is estimated by assuming that the action was taken; then the following actions for that instance are predicted

	Recall-*top*	Precision-*top*	F-score-*top*	Recall-*all*	Precision-*all*	F-score-*all*
Base	0.28	0.28	0.28	0.9	0.1	0.18
1stage	0.52	0.71	0.6	0.67	0.68	0.675
2stage	0.5	0.68	0.58	0.67	0.67	0.67
Base	0.0	0.0	0.0	0.62	0.002	0.004
1stage	0.15	0.26	0.19	0.23	0.17	0.2
2stage	0.26	0.65	0.37	0.3	0.55	0.39

Table 1: Test set results for the 3 systems on year completed (top) and architect name (bottom).

using H_{i-1} (line 8); and the complete sequence of actions is compared against the correct output using the loss function (line 9). Since the latter is only applied to complete sequences, it does not need to decompose over individual actions. We define the loss to be 0 when the relation extraction stage is correct and 1 otherwise. Therefore we do not need to know the labels for entity filtering, but we learn a classifier for it so that the relation extraction predictions are correct. Finally, the CSC training examples generated are added (line 10) and a new policy is learnt (line 11).

Since the losses are either 0 or 1, the CSC learning task is equivalent to ordinary classification learning. To learn the binary classifiers for each stage we implemented the adaptive regularization of weights (AROW) algorithm (Crammer et al., 2009) which scales to large datasets and handles sparse feature sets by adjusting the learning rate for each feature. In the first iteration, we do not have a learned policy, thus we assume a naive entity filter that accepts all candidate answers and a relation extractor that predicts the correct label.

5 Experiments

The relations used for evaluation are building-architect and building-completion_year, for the reasons given in Sec. 1. For each of the 138 listed historical buildings in Wikipedia,[1] we found the correct answers, resulting in 60 building-completion_year and 68 building-architect pairs. We split the data into two equal parts for training/development and testing. We then collected relevant web pages querying the web as described in Sec. 2. The queries were submitted to Bing via its Search API and the top 300 results for each query were obtained. We downloaded the corresponding pages and extracted their textual content with BoilerPipe (Kohlschütter et al., 2010). We then processed the texts using the Stanford CoreNLP toolkit.[2] We tried to match the question entity with tokens in each of the sentences, allowing for minor differences in tokenization, whitespace and capitalization. If a sentence contained the question entity and a candidate answer, we parsed it using the Klein and Manning (2002) parser. The instances generated were labeled using the distant supervision assumption, resulting in 974K and 4.5M labeled instances for the completion year and the architect relation, respectively.

We ran experiments with three systems; the jointly learned entity filtering-relation extraction approach using imitation learning (henceforth 2stage), the one-stage classification approach using the features for both entity filtering and relation extraction (henceforth 1stage), and a baseline that for each question entity returns all candidate answers for the relation ranked by the number of times they appeared with the question entity and ignoring all other information (henceforth Base). Following four-fold cross-validations experiment on the development data, we used 12 iterations for learning with DAGGER.

Each system returns a list of answers ranked according to the number of instances classified as positive for that answer. We used two evaluation modes. The first considers only the top-ranked answer (*top*), whereas the second considers all answers returned until either the correct one is found or they are exhausted (*all*). In *all* we define recall as the number of correct answers over the total number of question entities, and precision as the chance of finding the correct answer while traversing those returned.

Results by all models are reported for both relations in Table 1. A first observation is that the architect name relation is substantially harder to extract since all models achieve worse scores than for the completion year relation. More specifically, Base achieves respectable scores in *top* mode in completion year extraction, but it fails completely in architect name. This is due to the existence of many other names

[1] http://en.wikipedia.org/wiki/Category:Listed_buildings_in_Edinburgh
[2] http://nlp.stanford.edu/software/corenlp.shtml

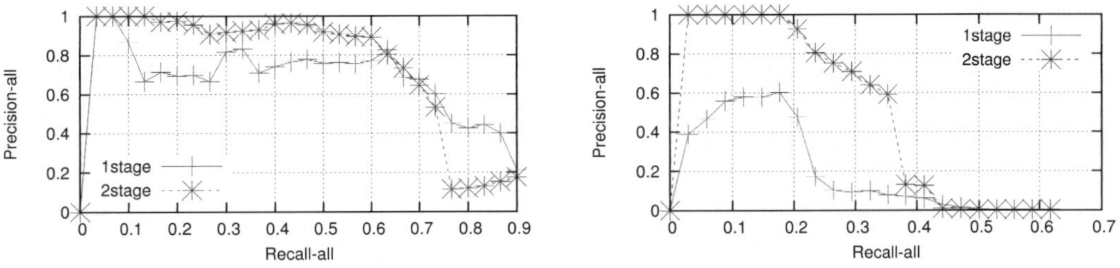

Table 2: Test set precision-recall curves in *all* mode for year completed (left) and architect name (right).

that appear more frequently together with a building than that of its architect, while the completion year is sometimes the number most frequently mentioned in the same sentence with the building. In addition, Base achieves the maximum possible *all* recall by construction, since if there is a sentence containing the correct answer for a question entity it will be returned. However this comes at a cost of low precision.

Both the machine-learned models improve upon Base substantially on both datasets, with the 2stage model being substantially better in architect name extraction, especially in terms of precision. In completion year extraction the differences are smaller, with 1stage being slightly better. These small differences are expected since recognizing completion years is much easier than recognizing architect names, thus learning a separate entity filtering model for them is less likely to be useful. Nevertheless, inspecting the weights learned by the 2stage model showed that some useful distinctions were learned, e.g. being preceded by the word "between" as in "built between 1849 and 1852" renders a number less likely to be a completion year. Finally, we examined the quality of the learned models further by generating precision-recall curves for the *all* mode by adjusting the classification thresholds used by 1stage and 2stage. As shown in the plots of Table 2, 2stage achieves higher precision than 1stage at most recall levels for both relations, with the benefits being more pronounced in the architect name relation. Summarizing these curves using average precision (Manning et al., 2008), the scores were 0.69 and 0.76 for the completion year, and 0.21 and 0.51 for the architect, for the 1stage and the 2stage models respectively, thus confirming the usefulness of separating the entity filtering features from relation extraction.

6 Discussion

While all the buildings considered in our experiments have a dedicated Wikipedia page, only a few had a sentence mentioning them together with the correct answer in that resource. Also, the architects who were the correct answers did not always have a dedicated Wikipedia page. Even though combining a search engine with distant supervision results in a highly imbalanced learning task, it increases the potential coverage of our system. In this process we rely on the keywords used in the queries in order to find pages containing the entities intended rather than synonymous ones, e.g. the keyword "building" helps avoid extracting sentences mentioning saints instead of churches. Nevertheless, building names such as churches named after saints were often ambiguous resulting in false positives.

Bunescu and Mooney (2007) also used a small seed set and a search engine, but they collected sentences via queries containing both the question and the answer entities, thus (unreallistically) assuming knowledge of all the correct answers. Instead we rely on simple heuristics to identify candidate answers. These heuristics are relation-dependent and different types of answers can be easily accommodated, e.g. in completed year relation they are single-token numbers. Finally, the entity filters learned jointly with relation extraction in our approach, while they perform a role similar to NER, they are learned so that they help avoid relation extraction errors and not to replace an actual NER system.

7 Conclusions

Our application-based setting has placed novel demands on relation extraction system trained with distant supervision, and in this paper we have shown that reasonable results can be obtained with only around 30 seed examples without requiring NER for pre-processing. Furthermore, we have demonstrated that learning entity filters and relation extraction jointly improves performance.

Acknowledgements

The research reported was conducted while the first author was at the University of Cambridge and funded by the European Community's Seventh Framework Programme (FP7/2007-2013) under grant agreement no. 270019 (SPACEBOOK project `www.spacebook-project.eu`).

References

Razvan Bunescu and Raymond Mooney. 2007. Learning to extract relations from the web using minimal supervision. In *Proceedings of the 45th Annual Meeting of the Association of Computational Linguistics*, pages 576–583.

Koby Crammer, Alex Kulesza, and Mark Dredze. 2009. Adaptive regularization of weight vectors. In *Advances in Neural Information Processing Systems 22*, pages 414–422.

Mark Craven and Johan Kumlien. 1999. Constructing biological knowledge-bases by extracting information from text sources. In *Proceedings of the 7th International Conference on Intelligent Systems for Molecular Biology*, pages 77–86.

Hal Daumé III, John Langford, and Daniel Marcu. 2009. Search-based structured prediction. *Machine Learning*, 75:297–325.

He He, Hal Daumé III, and Jason Eisner. 2013. Dynamic feature selection for dependency parsing. In *Proceedings of the 2013 Conference on Empirical Methods in Natural Language Processing*, pages 1455–1464, Seattle, October.

Raphael Hoffmann, Congle Zhang, Xiao Ling, Luke Zettlemoyer, and Daniel S. Weld. 2011. Knowledge-based weak supervision for information extraction of overlapping relations. In *Proceedings of the 49th Annual Meeting of the Association for Computational Linguistics*, pages 541–550.

Dan Klein and Chris Manning. 2002. Fast exact inference with a factored model for natural language parsing. In *Advances in Neural Information Processing Systems 15*, pages 3–10.

Christian Kohlschütter, Peter Fankhauser, and Wolfgang Nejdl. 2010. Boilerplate detection using shallow text features. In *Proceedings of the 3rd ACM International Conference on Web Search and Data Mining*, pages 441–450.

Xiao Ling and Daniel S. Weld. 2012. Fine-grained entity recognition. In *Proceedings of the 26th Conference on Artificial Intelligence*, pages 94–100.

Christopher D. Manning, Prabhakar Raghavan, and Hinrich Schtze. 2008. *Introduction to Information Retrieval.* Cambridge University Press, New York, NY, USA.

Mike Mintz, Steven Bills, Rion Snow, and Dan Jurafsky. 2009. Distant supervision for relation extraction without labeled data. In *Proceedings of the Joint Conference of the 47th Annual Meeting of the ACL and the 4th International Joint Conference on Natural Language Processing of the AFNLP*, pages 1003–1011.

Stéphane Ross, Geoffrey J. Gordon, and Drew Bagnell. 2011. A reduction of imitation learning and structured prediction to no-regret online learning. In *14th International Conference on Artificial Intelligence and Statistics*, pages 627–635.

Andreas Vlachos. 2012. An investigation of imitation learning algorithms for structured prediction. *Journal of Machine Learning Research Workshop and Conference Proceedings, Proceedings of the 10th European Workshop on Reinforcement Learning*, 24:143–154.

Limin Yao, Sebastian Riedel, and Andrew McCallum. 2010. Collective cross-document relation extraction without labelled data. In *Proceedings of the 2010 Conference on Empirical Methods in Natural Language Processing*, pages 1013–1023.

Xingxing Zhang, Jianwen Zhang, Junyu Zeng, Jun Yan, Zheng Chen, and Zhifang Sui. 2013. Towards accurate distant supervision for relational facts extraction. In *Proceedings of the 51st Annual Meeting of the Association for Computational Linguistics (Volume 2: Short Papers)*, pages 810–815, Sofia, Bulgaria, August. Association for Computational Linguistics.

A Comparative Study of Conversion Aided Methods for WordNet Sentence Textual Similarity

Muhidin Mohamed
EECE University of Birmingham,
Edgbaston, Birmingham, UK
Mam256@bham.ac.uk

M. Oussalah
EECE University of Birmingham,
Edgbaston, Birmingham, UK
M.Oussalah@bham.ac.uk

Abstract

In this paper, we present a comparison of three methods for taxonomic-based sentence semantic relatedness, aided with word parts of speech (PoS) conversion. We use WordNet ontology for determining word level semantic similarity while augmenting WordNet with two other lexicographical databases; namely Categorial Variation Database (CatVar) and Morphosemantic Database in assisting the word category conversion. Using a human annotated benchmark data set, all the three approaches achieved a high positive correlation reaching up to (r = 0.881647) with comparison to human ratings and two other baselines evaluated on the same benchmark data set.

1 Introduction

Sentence textual similarity is a crucial and a prerequisite subtask for many text processing and NLP tasks including text summarization, document classification, text clustering, topic detection, automatic question answering, automatic text scoring, plagiarism detection, machine translation, conversational agents among others (Ali, Ghosh, & Al-Mamun, 2009; Gomaa & Fahmy, 2013; Haque, Naskar, Way, Costa-Jussà, & Banchs, 2010; K. O'Shea, 2012; Osman, Salim, Binwahlan, Alteeb, & Abuobieda, 2012). There are two predominant approaches for sentence similarity: corpus-based and knowledge-based. The former utilises information exclusively derived from large corpora including word frequency of occurrence, and latent semantic analysis, to infer semantic similarity. On the other hand, Knowledge-based measures employ the intrinsic structure of a semantic network including its hierarchy to derive the semantic similarity. One of the commonly used knowledge networks for semantic similarity is WordNet. It is a hierarchical lexical database for English developed at Princeton University (Miller, 1995). The state of the art WordNet sentence similarity is harvested from pairing the constituent words of the two compared sentences. This is based on the intuition that similar sentences in meaning will indeed comprise semantically related words. However, these pairings only handle nouns and verbs as other part-of-speech (PoS) attributes are not accounted for in WordNet taxonomy. Taxonomic similarity is a conceptual relatedness derived from hyponymy/hypernymy relations of lexical ontologies. In this study, we use a group of WordNet semantic relations, e.g. synonymy, hyponymy, for similarity determination and for the approximation of noun equivalents of other PoS words.

In implementing the conversion aided methods, we adapted a publicly available package (Pedersen, Patwardhan, & Michelizzi, 2004) to measure word level similarity. We computed word similarities from word senses using Wu and Palmer's measure (Wu & Palmer, 1994) as given in expression 1.

$$Sim(w_1, w_2) = \max_{c_1 \in senses(w_1), c_2 \in senses(w_2)} \left(\frac{2 * depth(lcs(c_1, c_2))}{depth(c_1) + depth(c_2)}\right) \quad (1)$$

Where $\boldsymbol{lcs(c_i, c_j)}$ (lowest common subsumer) stands for the synset subsuming concepts $\boldsymbol{c_i}$ and $\boldsymbol{c_j}$ while depth $(\boldsymbol{c_i})$ indicates the number of nodes from concept $\boldsymbol{c_i}$ to the root node of the hierarchy.

Next, the above word-to-word semantic similarity is extended to sentence-to-sentence semantic similarity, say $\boldsymbol{S_i}$ and $\boldsymbol{S_j}$ using (Malik, Subramaniam, & Kaushik, 2007) like approach, where pairs of the same PoS tokens from the two sentences are evaluated.

$$Sim(S_i, S_j) = \frac{1}{2}\left[\frac{\sum_{w_1 \in S_i} \text{Max}_{w_2 \in S_j} Sim(w_1, w_2)}{|S_i|} + \frac{\sum_{w_1 \in S_j} \text{Max}_{w_2 \in S_i} Sim(w_1, w_2)}{|S_j|}\right], \; PoS(w_1) = PoS(w_2) \quad (2)$$

In (2), $Sim(w_1, w_2)$ stands for word level similarity measure in (1).

Nevertheless, for common natural language texts, it remains biased if only verbs and nouns are used to measure semantic relatedness ignoring other word categories such as adjectives, adverbs and named entities. To elaborate that, consider the following pair of semantically identical sentences with different word surface forms and classes.

S_1: He stated that the construction of the house is complete.

S_2: He said in a statement that the house is completely constructed.

Initial preprocessing tasks including tokenization, normalization, and stop-words removal reduce sentences to their semantic words with S_1 yielding (*state, construction, house, complete*) and (*statement, house, completely, construct*) for S_2. To optimize the semantic similarity of the two sentences, their scores from the word pairings need to be maximized regardless their associated part of speech. For S_1 and S_2, this is only achievable when words are paired as *(statement, state), (house, house), (construction, construct) and (complete, completely).* However, using quantification (2) yields a Sim(S_1,S_2) score of 0.543. This is justifiable as computing the similarity of the above first, third and fourth pairs, is out of reach using conventional WordNet measures due to each word pair falling in different PoS. To handle the above limitation, the idea advocated in this paper is to turn all non-noun PoS terms into corresponding noun expressions in order to enhance the pairing tasks.

The rationale behind the migration to noun category instead of other PoS categories relies on the inherent well elaborated properties of noun category in the taxonomical hierarchy, e.g., number of nouns is much more important than other attributes in most lexical databases, which increases the chance of finding noun-counterpart; WordNet 3 has a depth of 20 for nouns and 14 for verbs, which allows for much more elaborated hyponym/hypernym relations for instance. It is also the case that words in the lower layers of the deeper hierarchical taxonomy have more specific concepts which consequently yield a high semantic similarity (Li, McLean, Bandar, O'shea, & Crockett, 2006). This is again supported by the argument presented in (Bawakid & Oussalah, 2010).

The reasons stated above and WordNet limitation of parts of speech boundary motived the current study of word PoS conversion in an attempt to improve the measurement of taxonomic-based short text semantic similarity. In this respect, transforming all other primary word categories[1] of the previous example to nouns using CatVar (Habash & Dorr, 2003) aided conversion has raised the similarity from 0.543 to 0.86. Since the two sentences of the previous example are intuitively highly semantically related, the noun-conversion brings the sentence similarity closer to human judgement. This again highlights the importance of word PoS conversion to move freely beyond the barrier of PoS restriction. This paper aims to investigate three distinct word conversion schemes. Although, all the three approaches use WordNet for measuring the term level similarity, each stands on a distinct external lexical resource in converting word's category; namely, WordNet 3.0, the Categorial Variation Database (CatVar), and the Morphosemantic Database (Fellbaum, Osherson, & Clark, 2009).

CatVar is a lexical database containing word categorial variations for English lexemes sharing a common stem, e.g. $research_V$, $researcher_N$, $researchable_{AJ}$,. Likewise, Morphosematic Database is a WordNet-related linguistic resource that links morphologically related nouns and verbs in WordNet. Both aforementioned databases are solely utilized to aid the PoS conversion of three primary word classes to nouns. Contributions of this paper are two folded. First, we improved traditional WordNet sentence similarity by converting poorly or non-hierarchized word categories (e.g. verbs, adverbs and adjectives) to a class with well-structured and deep taxonomy (nouns) using WordNet relations, CatVar and Morphosemantic databases. Second, we have performed a comparison among the three PoS conversion techniques to discover the most appropriate supplementary database to WordNet.

2 Word Parts of Speech Conversion Methods

The two conversion methods aided with CatVar and Morphosemantics were performed by looking up the word to be converted from the corresponding database and replacing it with target category word. For example to convert the verb ***arouse***, a simple look-up database matching yields **arousal** as an equivalent noun to ***arouse*** in both databases (***arouse*** $\Rightarrow$ ***arousal***). However, WordNet aided conversion cannot be accomplished with a simple look up and replacement strategy due to the nature of its lexical organization that emphasises word semantics rather than their morphology. For this purpose, to con-

[1] Verbs, adjectives, adverbs

vert verb category into noun category, we designed a systematic four level conversion procedure starting with a verb surface form where the verb itself is checked for having noun form. If the latter fails, the second level investigates the synonyms of the verb senses, where each synset is checked whether a noun-form exists. If a noun member is found a replacement is issued, otherwise, another subsequent reasoning is applied. The third level differs from the previous two in that it goes down one level to the child node in the WordNet taxonomy following the hyponymy relation in which case the verb is converted by replacing it by the first encountered node containing the target category. Last but not least, the fourth level is based on moving one parent node up the taxonomy through the hypernymy relation where the first obtained noun is used as an approximate noun counterpart. Fig. 1 illustrates the WordNet aided conversion levels indicating an example of word conversion achieved at each level (see underneath the figure). On the other hand, derivation rules in WorldNet allow us to convert advert/adjective categories into their noun counterparts if available.

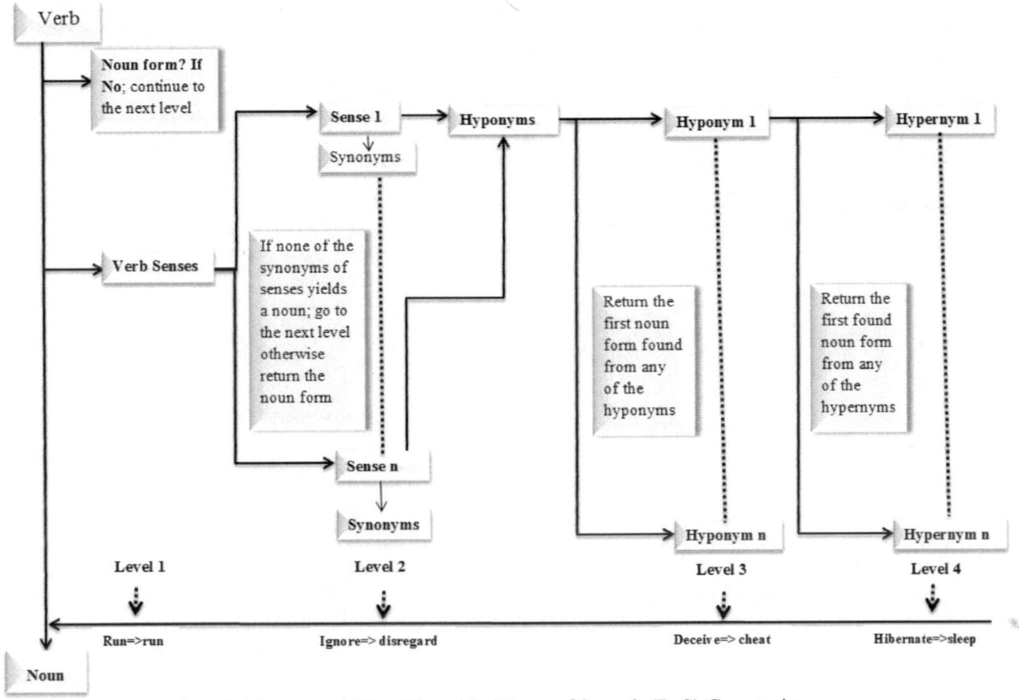

Fig. 1: The 4-level WordNet Aided Parts of Speech (PoS) Conversion

3 Implementation and Experiments

Figure 2 (a) depicts our layered implementation of the multiple conversion aided sentence semantic similarity. For every two sentences, we determine how closely the two are semantically related using scores between 1 and 0 with 1 indicating identical texts. Fig 1 (b) highlights a functional algorithm that summarizes the word category conversion process. The ***convert(w)*** function in the same algorithm performs the parts of speech conversion from the selected database depending on the active approach (A in Fig.2 (a)). All text pre-processing tasks including tokenization, parts of speech tagging, and stop words removal are implemented in layer 1. The second layer houses the three main word category conversion approaches in discussion. In each experimental run, only one approach is used depending on the choice of internally hardcoded system logic. The generated output from layer 2 is sentence text vectors having the same part of speech. These vectors are then fed into the Text Semantic Similarity Module to measure the similarity score using Wu and Palmer measure (Wu & Palmer, 1994) for word level similarity and WordNet taxonomy as an information source according to equations (1-2).

3.1 Data set

We conducted system experiments on a pilot benchmark data set created for measuring short-text semantic similarity (O'Shea, Bandar, Crockett, & McLean, 2008). It contains 65 sentence pairs with human similarity judgements assigned to each pair. During this data set creation, 32 graduate native speakers were assigned to score the degree of similarity using scores from 0 to 4 and following a guideline of semantic anchor (Charles, 2000) included in Table 2. To make the semantic anchors comply with our system generated scores (0 to 1), the scale points have been linearly transformed as indicated in the second column of the same table.

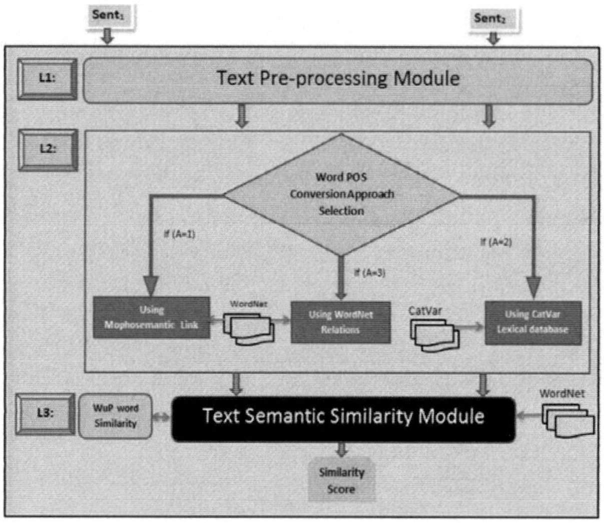

Algorithm1: Word Parts Of Speech Conversion

Input: sentence with different word classes;
Output: sentence with same word class(CWS);

S ← Sentence;
CWS← { };
C ← { }
W ← tokenize(S)
for each $w_i \in$ W **do**
  If w_i = inflected **then**
    w_i ← baseform(w_i)
  endif
  If (w_i not in targetcategory)
    cw← convert (w_i)
  endif
  CWS ← CWS {**cw**}
end for
return CWS

(a) (b)

Fig. 2: (a) Word POS conversion aided semantic similarity system; (b) Word parts of speech conversion Algorithm

Table 1: Semantic Anchors

Scale Points	Transformed Scale Points*	Semantic Anchor
0.0	0.0	The sentences are unrelated in meaning
1.0	0.25	The sentences are vaguely similar in meaning
2.0	0.5	The sentences are very much a like in meaning
3.0	0.75	The sentences are strongly related in meaning
4.0	1.0	The sentences are identical in meaning

3.2 Results and Evaluation

Our evaluation for all three conversion assisted systems is centered around the human judgements. Human ratings reflect the extent to which every two sentences are semantically related from the human perception. A comparison of our conversion aided methods (*TW, CwW, CwM, CwC*) and the findings of two baseline methods (*STASIS, LSA*) is presented in Table 2. The notations *TW, CwW, CwM, CwC* stand for, traditional WordNet, conversion with WordNet, conversion with Morphosemantics and conversion with CatVar respectively. We selected the baselines because of their fitness for purpose and their evaluation on the same benchmark data. *STASIS,* thoroughly described in (Li, et al., 2006), is a textual similarity measure combining taxonomy and word order information to compute the semantic relatedness for two sentences. While LSA (latent sematic analysis) (Deerwester et. al, 1990) is a corpus-based measure developed for indexing and retrieval of text documents but later adapted for tasks including sentence similarity. In LSA, texts are represented as a matrix, of high dimensional semantic vectors, which is then transformed using Singular Value Decomposition (SVD); namely, $A = TSD^T$, where A is a term-document matrix, S is the diagonal matrix of the Singular Value Decomposition, while T and D are left and right singular vectors with orthogonal columns. As pointed out, the results obtained in (J. O'Shea, Bandar, Crockett, & McLean, 2008) have been compared to our experimental results. Due to the space limitation, results of only 10 randomly selected sentence pairs from the benchmark data set are listed in Table 2 with the second column being the human ratings.

Table 2. Human, STASIS, LSA, TW, CwW, CwM and CwC similarity scores for 10 sentence pairs

Sentence Pair	Human	STASIS	LSA	TW	CwW	CwM	CwC
1.cord:smile	0.01	0.329	0.51	0.362	0.49	0.57	0.667
9.asylum:fruit	0.005	0.209	0.505	0.430	0.43	0.506	0.522
17.coast:forest	0.063	0.356	0.575	0.616	0.738	0.80	0.791
29.bird:woodland	0.013	0.335	0.505	0.465	0.583	0.665	0.665
33.hill:woodland	0.145	0.59	0.81	0.826	0.826	0.826	0.826
57.forest:woodland	0.628	0.7	0.75	0.709	0.804	0.867	0.867
58.implement:tool	0.59	0.753	0.83	0.781	0.744	0.905	0.885
59.cock:rooster	0.863	1	0.985	1	1	1	1
61.cushion:pillow	0.523	0.662	0.63	0.636	0.637	0.723	0.842
65.gem: jewel	0.653	0.831	0.86	0.717	0.745	0.793	0.778

To measure the strength of the linear association measured in terms of the correlation coefficients *r*, between the score of each conversion aided method and the human judgements, are computed and presented in Table 3 using equation 3 where ***n*** is the number of sentence pairs while $\boldsymbol{m_i}$ and $\boldsymbol{h_i}$ represent machine and human scores, respectively, for the ith pair.

$$r = \frac{n\sum_i h_i m_i - \sum_i h_i \sum_i m_i}{\sqrt{(n\sum_i h_i^2 - (\sum_i h_i)^2)}\sqrt{(n\sum_i m_i^2 - (\sum_i m_i)^2)}} \quad (3)$$

The performances of all the three methods gradually excel with an increasing shared semantic strength between the sentence pairs. However, for the less related sentence pairs, it is evident that the human perception of similarity is more strict than the loose definition of similarity based on lexical concepts and hierarchical taxonomy. Table 2 shows that all the three conversion aided methods considerably improve semantic scores over the traditional WordNet (TW). Out of the three schemes, CatVar-aided conversion establishes the highest semantic correlation between the sentence pairs corroborating the hypothesis that CatVar can be used as a supplementary resource to WordNet. Overall, scores of correlation coefficients of the developed approaches with the baseline methods; STASIS and LSA and human judgements indicate that CatVar-based conversion provides best performance. On the other hand, the correlation coefficients (expression 3) between our conversions aided schemes and the two compared benchmark methods along with the human judgements, summarized in Table 3, shows that statistically speaking, latent semantic analysis (LSA) provides the best consistency with WordNet-based similarity measures.

Table 3: Correlations Coefficients (r) between machine and human scores

	CwW	*CwM*	*CwC*	*STASIS*	*LSA*
Human	0.729826	0.830984	0.881647	0.816	0.838
STASIS	0.771874	0.851675	0.872939	--	0.76
LSA	0.804518	0.875024	0.822453	0.76	--

In order to visualize the effect of correlation coefficient across sentence pairs, Fig. 3 illustrates the association between the human ratings and each of the achieved results. It is evident that all the three relationships follow a positive linear trend with slightly varying but strong correlation with the human judgements and without outliers. For those sentence pairs which are either strongly related or identical in meaning, there is a high agreement between the human evaluation and machine assessment for semantic similarity. The results also confirm that CatVar aided conversion yields a strong positive correlation with the human rating.

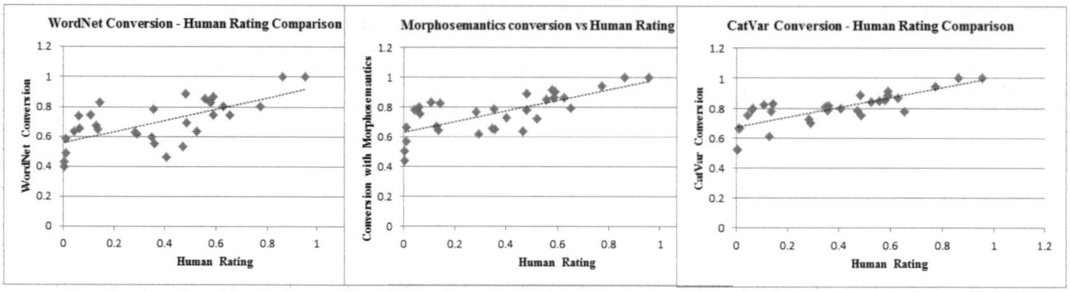

Fig. 3: Relationships between the obtained results and human judgements for the benchmark data set

4 Conclusion

To improve the accuracy of capturing semantic textual relatedness, we carried out word parts of speech conversion by augmenting two lexical databases; CatVar and Morphosemantics to traditional WordNet similarity. Our comparative analysis with human judgements and two baseline systems found that WordNet taxonomy can be supplemented with other linguistic resources, such as CatVar, to enhance the measurement of sentence semantic similarity. The findings revealed that the word parts of speech conversion captures the sematic correlation between two pieces of text in a way that brings closer to human perception. As a future work, we plan to improve the suggested conversion aided similarity measures and apply them on various large scale data set.

References

Ali, M., Ghosh, M. K., & Al-Mamun, A. (2009). *Multi-document Text Summarization: SimWithFirst Based Features and Sentence Co-selection Based Evaluation.* Paper presented at the Future Computer and Communication, 2009. ICFCC 2009. International Conference on.

Bawakid, A., & Oussalah, M. (2010). *A semantic-based text classification system.* Paper presented at the Cybernetic Intelligent Systems (CIS), 2010 IEEE 9th International Conference on.

Charles, W. G. (2000). Contextual correlates of meaning. *Applied Psycholinguistics, 21*(04), 505-524.

Deerwester et. al, S. C. (1990). Indexing by latent semantic analysis. *JASIS, 41*(6), 391-407.

Fellbaum, C., Osherson, A., & Clark, P. E. (2009). Putting semantics into WordNet's" morphosemantic" links *Human Language Technology. Challenges of the Information Society* (pp. 350-358): Springer.

Gomaa, W. H., & Fahmy, A. A. (2013). A Survey of text similarity approaches. *International Journal of Computer Applications, 68*(13), 13-18.

Habash, N., & Dorr, B. (2003). *A categorial variation database for English.* Paper presented at the Proceedings of the 2003 Conference of the North American Chapter of the Association for Computational Linguistics on Human Language Technology-Volume 1.

Haque, R., Naskar, S. K., Way, A., Costa-Jussà, M. R., & Banchs, R. E. (2010). *Sentence similarity-based source context modelling in pbsmt.* Paper presented at the Asian Language Processing (IALP), 2010 International Conference on.

Li, Y., McLean, D., Bandar, Z. A., O'shea, J. D., & Crockett, K. (2006). Sentence similarity based on semantic nets and corpus statistics. *Knowledge and Data Engineering, IEEE Transactions on, 18*(8), 1138-1150.

Malik, R., Subramaniam, L. V., & Kaushik, S. (2007). *Automatically Selecting Answer Templates to Respond to Customer Emails.* Paper presented at the IJCAI.

Miller, G. A. (1995). WordNet: a lexical database for English. *Communications of the ACM, 38*(11), 39-41.

O'Shea, J., Bandar, Z., Crockett, K., & McLean, D. (2008). Pilot short text semantic similarity benchmark data set: Full listing and description. *Computing.*

O'Shea, J., Bandar, Z., Crockett, K., & McLean, D. (2008). A comparative study of two short text semantic similarity measures *Agent and Multi-Agent Systems: Technologies and Applications* (pp. 172-181): Springer.

O'Shea, K. (2012). An approach to conversational agent design using semantic sentence similarity. *Applied Intelligence, 37*(4), 558-568.

Osman, A. H., Salim, N., Binwahlan, M. S., Alteeb, R., & Abuobieda, A. (2012). An improved plagiarism detection scheme based on semantic role labeling. *Applied Soft Computing, 12*(5), 1493-1502.

Pedersen, T., Patwardhan, S., & Michelizzi, J. (2004). *WordNet:: Similarity: measuring the relatedness of concepts.* Paper presented at the Demonstration Papers at HLT-NAACL 2004.

Wu, Z., & Palmer, M. (1994). *Verbs semantics and lexical selection.* Paper presented at the Proceedings of the 32nd annual meeting on Association for Computational Linguistics.

Word Clustering Based on Un-LP Algorithm

Jiguang Liang[1], Xiaofei Zhou[1], Yue Hu[1], Li Guo[1*], Shuo Bai[1,2]
[1]National Engineering Laboratory for Information Security Technologies,
Institute of Information Engineering, Chinese Academy of Sciences,
Beijing 100190, China
[2]Shanghai Stock Exchange, Shanghai 200120, China
{liangjiguang, zhouxiaofei, huyue, guoli, baishuo}@iie.ac.cn

Abstract

Word clustering which generalizes specific features cluster words in the same syntactic or semantic categories into a group. It is an effective approach to reduce feature dimensionality and feature sparseness which are clearly useful for many NLP applications. This paper proposes an unsupervised label propagation algorithm (Un-LP) for word clustering which uses multi-exemplars to represent a cluster. Experiments on a synthetic 2D dataset show the strong ability of self-correcting of the proposed algorithm. Besides, the experimental results on 20NG demonstrate that our algorithm outperforms the conventional cluster algorithms.

1 Introduction

Word clustering is the task of the division of words into a certain number of clusters (groups or categories). Each cluster is required to consist of words that are similar to one another in syntactic or semantic construct and dissimilar to words in distinctive groups. Word clustering generalizes specific features by considering the common characteristics and ignoring the specific characteristics among the individual features. It is an effective approach to reduce feature dimensionality and feature sparseness (Han et al., 2005).

Recently, word clustering offers great potential for various useful NLP applications. Several studies have addressed dependency parsing (Koo et al., 2008; Sagae and Gordon, 2009). Momtazi and Klakow (2009) propose a word clustering approach to improve the performance of sentence retrieval in Question Answering (QA) systems. Wu et al. (2010) present an approach to integrate word clustering information into the process of unsupervised feature selection. Sun et al. (2011) use large-scale word clustering for a semi-supervised relation extraction system. It also contributes to word sense disambiguation (Jin et al., 2007), named entity recognition (Turian et al., 2010), part-of-speech tagging (Candito and Seddah, 2010) and machine translation (Uszkoreit and Brants, 2008; Jeff et al., 2011).

This paper presents an unsupervised algorithm for word clustering based on a probabilistic transition matrix. Given a text document dataset, a list of words is generated by removing stop words and very unfrequent words. Each word is required to be represented by the documents in the dataset, which results in a co-occurrence matrix. By calculating the similarity of words, a word similarity graph with transition (propagation) probabilities as weight edges is created. Then, a new kind word clustering algorithm, based on label propagation, is applied.

The remaining parts of this paper are organized as follows: Section 2 formulates word clustering problem in the context of unsupervised learning. Then we describe the word clustering algorithm in Section 3 and present our experiments in Section 4. Finally we conclude our work in Section 5.

2 Problem setup

Assume that we have a corpus with N documents denoted by $D = \{d_1, d_2, \cdots, d_N\}$; each document in the corpus consists of a list of words denoted by $d_i = \{w_1, w_2, \cdots, w_{N_d}\}$ where each w_i is an item from a vocabulary index with V distinct terms denoted by $W = \{v_1, v_2, \cdots, v_V\}$ and N_d is the document

Algorithm 1 Semi-supervised LP Algorithm

Input:
$W_l = \{v_i\}_{i=1}^{l}$ labeled data
$W_u = \{v_i\}_{i=u}^{V}$ unlabeled data
$\overline{T} = \{T_{ij}\}\ 1 \le i, j \le V$ transition matrix
Output: Y_U
Begin
Row-normalize T by $\overline{T}_{ij} = T_{ij} / \sum_{k=1}^{V} T_{ik}$
While not converged **do**
  Propagate the labels by $Y^{t+1} = \overline{T} Y^t$
  Row-normalize Y^{t+1}
  Clamp the labeled data
End while
End
Return Y_U

Algorithm 2 Unsupervised LP Word Clustering

Input:
$W = \{v_i\}_{i=1}^{u}\ (u = V)$ unlabeled words
$\overline{T}_{uu} = \{T_{ij}\}\ 1 \le i, j \le V$ transition matrix
Output:
$\Lambda = \{(\Lambda_1, \Lambda_2, \cdots, \Lambda_L\}$ word-clusters
Begin
$\{V_L^0, Y_L, \overline{T}_{ul}^{0}\} = initialization(W)$
While not converged **do**
  $Y_U^{t+1} = Semi - LP(V_L^t, Y_L^t, \overline{T}_{ul}^{0}, \overline{T}_{uu})$
  $\Lambda^{t+1} = partition\_cluster(Y_U^{t+1})$
  $\{V_L^{t+1}, \overline{T}_{ul}^{t+1}\} = update(\Lambda^{t+1})$
End while
End
Return Λ^{t+1}

length. We define the vector of word v_i in the vocabulary to be $v_i =< v_{id_1}, v_{id_2}, \cdots, v_{id_N} >$. This allows us to define a $V \times N$ word-document matrix WD for the vocabularies. WD_{ij} is equal to 1 if $v_i \in d_j$ and equal to 0 otherwise. Then we take these words as the vertices of a connected graph. In this paper, we define the edge weight ω_{ij} as the co-occurrence frequency between v_i and v_j. Obviously, we expect that larger edge weights allow labels to travel through more easily. So we define a $V \times V$ probabilistic transition matrix T where $T_{ij} = P(v_j \rightarrow v_i) = \omega_{ij} / \sum_{k=1}^{V} \omega_{kj}$.

The L value which is used to represent the number of word clusters is specified. We define a $V \times L$ label matrix Y. Clearly, $y_i \in Y$ represents the label probability distributions of word v_i and $Y_i^* = argmax\ Y_{ik}(0 < k \le L)$ is its cluster label. For example, suppose $L = 3$ and a word v has a label distribution $y =< 0.1, 0.8, 0.1 >$, it implies that v belongs to the second class.

3 Unsupervised LP Word Clustering

Label propagation (Zhu and Ghahramani, 2002) is a semi-supervised algorithm (Semi-LP) which needs labeled data. Let $\{(v_1, y_1), \cdots, (v_l, y_l)\}$ be labeled data, $\{(v_{l+1}, y_{l+1}), \cdots, (v_{l+u}, y_{l+u})\}$ be unlabeled ones where $l + u = V$, $Y_L = [y_1, , \cdots, y_l]^T$ and $Y_U = [y_{l+1}, \cdots, y_{l+u}]^T$. Y_U is un-known and $l << u$. The label propagation algorithm is summarized in Algorithm 1.

In clustering problems, the goal is to select a set of exemplars from a dataset that are representative of the dataset and each cluster is represented by one and only one exemplar (Krause and Gomes, 2010). However, these exemplars are just all Semi-LP needs for clustering. LP lacks labeled data when is used for unsupervised learning. In this paper, we are interested in partitioning words into several clusters without any label priori using unsupervised LP (Un-LP) algorithm. Firstly we randomly select K ($K \ge L$, usually K is a multiple of L) words to construct an exemplar set $E = \{E_i\}_{i=1}^{K}$ which is different from the conventional exemplar-based cluster algorithms, assign class labels to them and construct the corresponding probabilistic transition matrix $\overline{T}_{ul}^{0}$ ($initialization$). These exemplars are considered as labeled words and the rest $U = W - E$ are unlabeled words. $\overline{T}_{ul}$ is the probability of transition from unlabeled words to labeled ones. At this step, it needs the assurance that each class could be represented by at least one exemplar and each exemplar could only be assigned one class label.

Now the connected weighted graph consists of two parts: $G = (E \cup U, \overline{T}_{ul} \cup \overline{T}_{uu})$ where $\overline{T}_{uu}$ is the transition probability between unlabeled words. Next, our algorithm iterates between the following three steps: given a set of LP parameters, we first propagate labels to unlabeled words with the initial label distributions and get the corresponding labels ($Semi - LP$). Then, these derived label distributions are used to guide the partitioning of unlabeled data ($partition\_cluster$) to L clusters. We use residual sum of squares (RSS) to choose the most centrally located words and replace the old exemplars that represent the cluster. Specifically, for a word cluster $c_i = \{v_1, \cdots v_n\}$, $RSS_i = \sum_{j=1}^{n} \omega_{ij}$. Then we sort RSS_i $(0 < i < n)$ and update exemplars by the words with bigger RSS for this cluster ($update$). All of the above steps, summarized in Algorithm 2, are iterated until convergence.

4 Experiment

4.1 Experimental Setup

To demonstrate properties of our proposed algorithm we investigate both a synthetic dataset and a real-world dataset. Figure 1(a) shows the synthetic dataset. For a real world example we test Un-LP on a subset of 20 Newsgroups (20NG) dataset which is preprocessed by removing common stop-words and stemming. We use the classes *atheism*, *hardware*, *hockey* and *space* for test and randomly select 300 samples from each class as the test dataset in this section. However, 20NG is not suited for word clustering evaluation. So, firstly, we reconstruct it by pair-wise testing which is a specification-based testing criterion. Then we can obtain six ($C_4^2 = 6$) pairwise subsets represented by $\{D_1, \cdots, D_6\}$. In order to facilitate the evaluation, we use those words that only occur in one class for clustering.

4.2 Exemplar Self-correction

This multi-step iterative method is simple to implement and surprisingly effective even with wrong initial labeled data. To illustrate the point, we describe a simulated dataset with two-moon pattern. Obviously, the points in one moon should be more similar to each other than the points across the moons as shown in Figure 1(b). During the initialization phase, four points in the lower moon are selected and assigned with different labels. The exemplars of the upper moon are mis-labeled as shown in Figure 1(c). In the next five iteration steps, exemplars have been gradually moved to the center of the upper moon. Finally, when $t \geq 5$ Un-LP converges to a fixed assignment, which achieves an ideal cluster result.

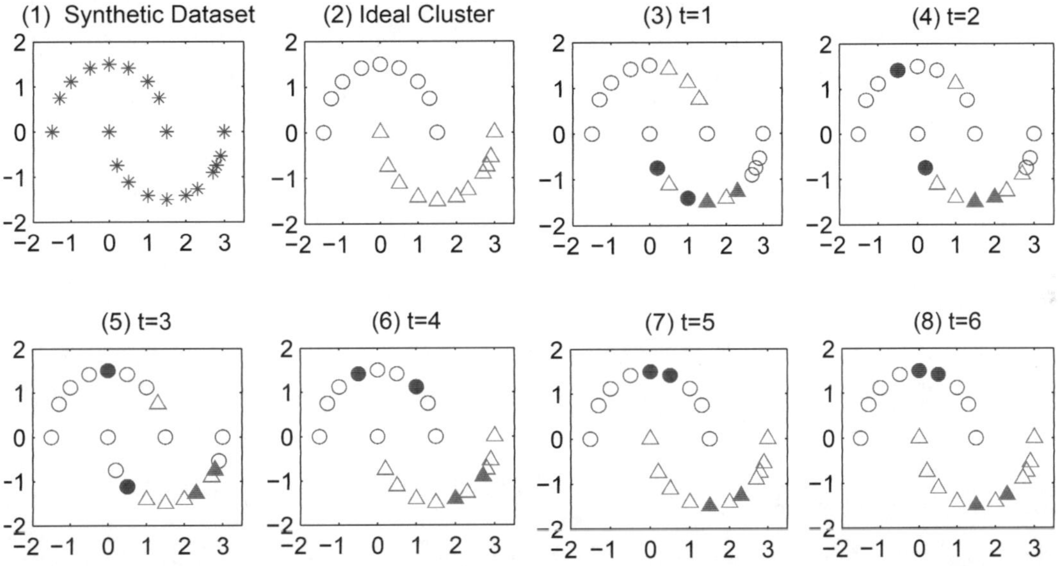

Figure 1: Clustering result of unsupervised LP clustering algorithm on two-moon pattern dataset. (a) Two-moon pattern dataset without any labeled points, (b) ideal clustering results. The convergence process of unsupervised LP with t from 1 to 6 is shown from (c) to (h). Solid points are labeled data that are selected to represent the clusters.

4.3 Word Clustering Performance

This section provides empirical evidence that the proposed algorithm performs well in the problem of word clustering. Figure 2 shows the mean precisions and recalls over 10 runs of the baseline algorithms as well as Un-LP.

From Figure 2, it can be clearly observed that Un-LP ($K/L = 5$) yields the best performance, followed by Semi-LP with 20 labeled words. In general, the recalls with k-means and k-medoids are higher, while the precisions are much lower. Figure 2 also shows the results of other two semi-supervised word

Cluster1	Cluster2	Cluster3	Cluster4
Atheism	Hardware	Hockey	Space
geode **religiously** **benefactor** *meng* stacker *mcl* **mormon** madden **mythology** *timmons* *cbnewsj* **agnostics** *fanatism* *engr* *chade* *tan* *falsifiable* *existed* *ucsb* *sentence*	**driver** **soundblaster** **cards** isbn **manufacturer** portal prize **mastering** **connectors** **floppies** dock **adapter** **multimedia** **installing** bowman *configure* *physchem* *jumpers* **motherboardsfdisk** **seagate**	**goalies** bug *hfd* *johansson* breton **scorers** *carpenter* *stevens* *smythe* *janney* *fleury* *vancouver* *stl* *cheveldae* *selanne* *winnipeg* *canadiens* *bure* *nyr* *capitals*	hub **atom** *aug* *larson* *sts* **orbital** skydive parity **accelerations** *desire* *anniversary* *projects* digital *protection* atari **temperatures** *voyagers* *zoology* *updated* *teflon*

Table 1: Top-20 words extracted by unsupervised LP word cluster algorithm.

clustering algorithms, PCK-means (Basu et al., 2004) and MPCK-means (Bilenko et al., 2004) with 200 must-link and cannot-link constraints. Also when comparing these unsupervised and semi-supervised approaches previously mentioned, we can find that our unsupervised algorithm consistently achieves significantly better results. Therefore, unsupervised LP seems to be a more reasonable algorithm design in terms of word clustering.

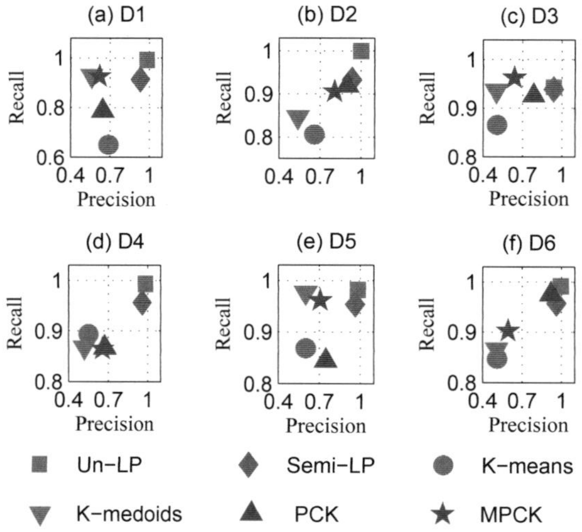

Figure 2: Precision vs. recall of clustering results on 20NG where $D_1 = \{atheism$ vs. $hardware\}$, $D_2 = \{atheism$ vs. $hockey\}$, $D_3 = \{atheism$ vs. $space\}$, $D_4 = \{hardware$ vs. $hcokey\}$, $D_5 = \{hardware$ vs. $space\}$ and $D_6 = \{hockey$ vs. $space\}$.

4.4 Effect of exemplar number e

We now investigate how the number of exemplar (e) for each cluster affects the clustering. In particular, we are interested in performance under conditions when the number of exemplar grows - which is the motivation for using more than one exemplars to represent a cluster. From Figure 3, we can observe that when more words are labeled, Semi-LP shows further improvement in F-value. However, the changes for PCK-means and MPCK-means are not obvious. Interestingly, even with the number of labeled data growing, Semi-LP still performs worse than Un-LP. As is shown in Figure 3, Un-LP benefits much from multi-exemplars ($e \geq 2$). For D4, Un-LP is capable of achieving 99.58% in F-value when $e = 7$, obtaining 21.32% improvement over the baseline ($e = 1$). This indicates that our algorithm leverages the additional exemplars effectively.

4.5 Case Study

We conduct an experiment to illustrate the characteristics of the proposed algorithm in this subsection. We cluster the words in all the four domain datasets and select the most representative words for each cluster by sorting y_i. In the experiment, we set $L = 4$ in order to match the class number of the dataset. Table 1 shows top-20 representative words for each cluster, where the bold words are the ones

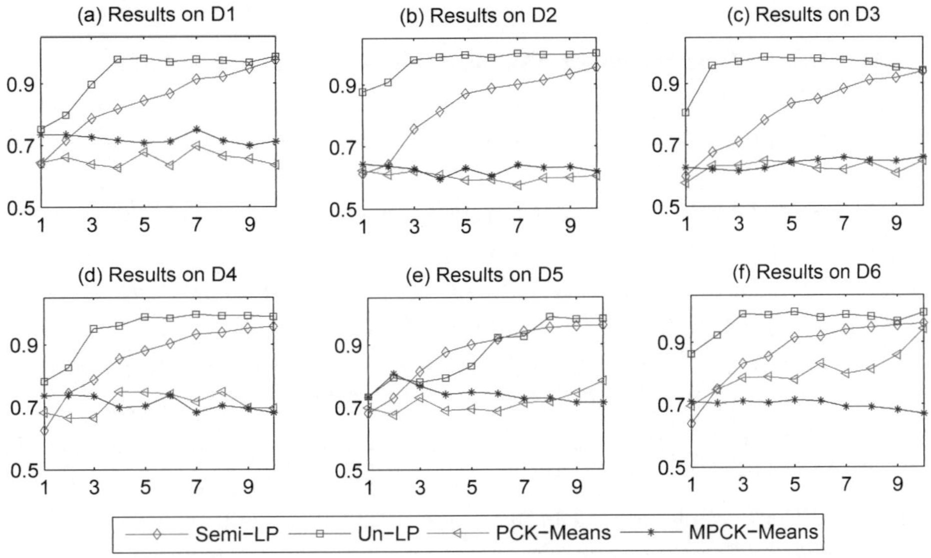

Figure 3: Results on 20NG where X-axis is e, Y-axis is F-value.

domain	*meng*	*configure*	*johansson*	*aug*	geode	isbn	bug	parity
Atheism	100.00%	0	0	0	0	91.67%	89.47%	0
Hardware	0	90.91%	0	0	0	0	10.53%	66.67%
Hockey	0	9.09%	100.00%	0	0	8.33%	0	0
Space	0	0	0	100.00%	100.00%	0	0	33.33%

Table 2: Distributions of the incorrect words partitioned by the literal meaning.

with correct cluster label inferencing from the literal meaning. We observe that the accuracy of word clustering on 20NG is very low (28.75%), which is at variance with the preceding conclusion. One reason is that words in 20NG are stemmed, so, from Table 1 it can be clearly seen that there are some non-English words (e.g., ”mcl”, ”hfd”, ”stl”, etc.) that don't have actual meanings.

In order to gain further insights into the reasons, the distributions of these incorrect words have been made in statistics. Partial results are shown in Table 2. From the distributions, we can find that many words marked in italics in Table 1 have been correctly clustered, although they have nothing to do with corresponding class in the literal meaning. Taking these words into account, the accuracy can reach 81.25% which demonstrates once again the effectiveness of Un-LP word clustering algorithm.

5 Conclusion

In this paper, we propose an unsupervised label propagation algorithm to tackle the problem of word clustering. The proposed algorithm uses a similarity graph based on co-occurrence information to encourage similar words to have similar cluster labels. One of the advantages of this algorithm is that it uses multi-exemplars to represent a cluster, which can significantly improve the clustering results.

Acknowledgements

This work was supported by Strategic Priority Research Program of Chinese Academy of Sciences (XDA06030602), National Nature Science Foundation of China (No. 61202226), National 863 Program (No. 2011AA010703), IIE Program (No.Y3Z0062201).

References

Basu S, Bilenko M, Mooney R J. 2004. A probabilistic framework for semi-supervised clustering. In *Proceedings of SIGKDD*, pages 59-68.

Bilenko M, Basu S, Mooney R J. 2004. Integrating constraints and metric learning in semi-supervised clustering. In *Proceedings of ICML.*

Blei D M, Ng A Y, Jordan M I. 2003. Latent dirichlet allocation. *The Journal of machine Learning research*, pages 993-1022.

Candito M, Seddah D. 2010. Parsing word clusters. In *Proceedings of the NAACL HLT 2010 First Workshop on Statistical Parsing of Morphologically-Rich Languages*, pages 76-84.

Han H, Manavoglu E, Zha H, et al. 2005. Rule-based word clustering for document metadata extraction. In *Proceedings of the 2005 ACM symposium on Applied computing*, pages 1049-1053.

Jeff M A, Matsoukas S, Schwartz R. 2011. Improving Low-Resource Statistical Machine Translation with a Novel Semantic Word Clustering Algorithm. In *Proceedings of the MT Summit XIII.*

Jin P, Sun X, Wu Y, et al. 2007. Word clustering for collocation-based word sense disambiguation. *Computational Linguistics and Intelligent Text Processing*, pages 267-274.

Koo T, Carreras X, Collins M. 2008. Simple semi-supervised dependency parsing. In *Proceedings of ACL-HLT*, pages 595-603.

Krause A, Gomes R G. 2010. Budgeted nonparametric learning from data streams. In *Proceedings of ICML*, pages 391-398.

Momtazi S, Klakow D. 2009. A word clustering approach for language model-based sentence retrieval in question answering systems. In *Proceedings of CIKM*, pages 1911-1914.

Sagae K, Gordon A S. 2009. Clustering words by syntactic similarity improves dependency parsing of predicate-argument structures. In *Proceedings of the 11th International Conference on Parsing Technologies*, pages 192-201.

Sun A, Grishman R, Sekine S. 2011. Semi-supervised relation extraction with large-scale word clustering. In *Proceedings of ACL*, pages 521-529.

Turian J, Ratinov L, Bengio Y. 2010. Word representations: a simple and general method for semi-supervised learning. In *Proceedings of ACL*, pages 384-394.

Uszkoreit J, Brants T. 2008. Distributed Word Clustering for Large Scale Class-Based Language Modeling in Machine Translation. In *Proceedings of ACL*, pages 755-762.

Wu Q, Ye Y, Ng M, et al. 2010. Exploiting word cluster information for unsupervised feature selection *Trends in Artificial Intelligence*, pages 292-303.

Zhu X, Ghahramani Z. 2002. Learning from labeled and unlabeled data with label propagation. *Technical Report CMU-CALD-02-107, Carnegie Mellon University.*

Zhu X, Ghahramani Z, Lafferty J. 2003. Semi-supervised learning using gaussian fields and harmonic functions. In *Proceedings of ICML*, pages 912-919.

Mining temporal footprints from Wikipedia

Michele Filannino
School of Computer Science
The University of Manchester
Manchester, M13 9PL, UK
filannim@cs.man.ac.uk

Goran Nenadic
School of Computer Science
The University of Manchester
Manchester, M13 9PL, UK
g.nenadic@manchester.ac.uk

Abstract

Discovery of temporal information is key for organising knowledge and therefore the task of extracting and representing temporal information from texts has received an increasing interest. In this paper we focus on the discovery of temporal footprints from encyclopaedic descriptions. Temporal footprints are time-line periods that are associated to the existence of specific concepts. Our approach relies on the extraction of date mentions and prediction of lower and upper boundaries that define temporal footprints. We report on several experiments on persons' pages from Wikipedia in order to illustrate the feasibility of the proposed methods.

1 Introduction

Temporal information, like dates, durations, time stamps etc., is crucial for organising both structured and unstructured data. Recent developments in the natural language community show an increased interest in systems that can extract temporal information from text and associate it to other concepts and events. The main aim is to detect and represent the temporal flow of events narrated in a text. For example, the TempEval challenge series (Verhagen et al., 2007; Verhagen et al., 2010; UzZaman et al., 2013) provided a number of tasks that have resulted in several temporal information extraction systems that can reliably extract complex temporal expressions from various document types (UzZaman and Allen, 2010; Llorens et al., 2010; Bethard, 2013; Filannino et al., 2013).

In this paper we investigate the extraction of *temporal footprints* (Kant et al., 1998): continuous periods on the time-line that temporally define a concept's existence. For example, the temporal footprint of people lies between their birth and death, whereas temporal footprint of a business company is a period between its constitution and closing or acquisition (see Figure 1 for examples). Such information would be useful in supporting several knowledge extraction and discovery tasks. A question answering system, for example, could spot temporally implausible questions (e.g. *What computer did Galileo Galilei use for his calculations?* or *Where did Blaise Pascal meet Leonardo Da Vinci?*), or re-rank candidate answers with respect to their temporal plausibility (e.g. *British politicians during the Age of Enlightenment*). Similarly, temporal footprints can be used to identify inconsistencies in knowledge bases.

Temporal footprints are in some cases easily accessible by querying Linked Data resources (e.g. DB-Pedia, YAGO or Freebase) (Rula et al., 2014), large collections of data (Talukdar et al., 2012) or by directly analysing Wikipedia info-boxes (Nguyen et al., 2007; Etzioni et al., 2008; Wu et al., 2008; Ji and Grishman, 2011; Kuzey and Weikum, 2012). However, the research question we want to address in this paper is whether it is possible to automatically approximate the temporal footprint of a concept only by analysing its encyclopaedic description rather than using such conveniently structured information.

This paper is organised as follows: Section 2 describes our approach and four different strategies to predict temporal footprints. Section 3 provides information about how we collected the data for the experiments, and Section 4 presents and illustrates the results.

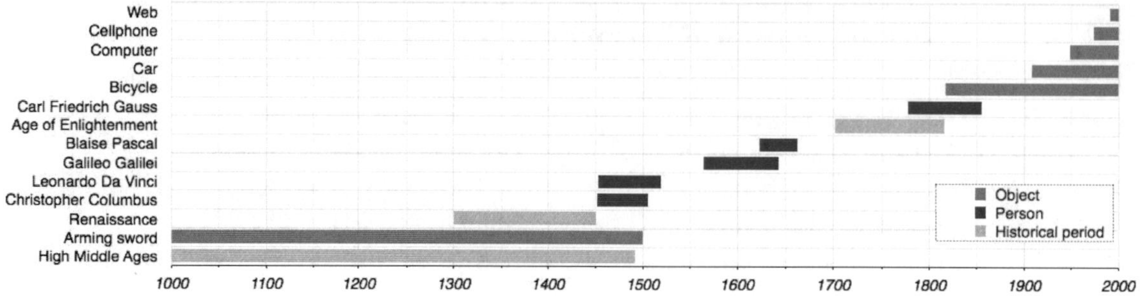

Figure 1: Examples of temporal footprints of objects, people and historical periods.

2 Methodology

In order to identify a temporal footprint for a given entity, we propose to predict its lower and upper bound using temporal expressions appearing in the associated text. The approach has three steps: (1) extracting mentions of temporal expressions, (2) filtering outliers from the obtained probability mass function of these mentions, and (3) fitting a normal distribution to this function. This process is controlled by three parameters we introduce and describe below. We restrict temporal footprints to the granularity of years.

2.1 Temporal expression extraction (TEE)

For each concept we extract all the dates from its associated textual content (e.g. a Wikipedia page). There are numerous ways to extract mentions of dates, but we use (a) regular expressions that search for mentions of full years (e.g. sequence of four digits that start with '1' or '2' (e.g. *1990*, *1067* or *2014*) — we refer to this as TEE RegEx; (b) a more sophisticated temporal expression extraction system, which can also extract implicit date references, such as *"a year after"* or *"in the same period"*, along with the explicit ones and, for this reason, would presumably be able to extract more dates. As temporal expression extraction system we used HeidelTime (Strötgen et al., 2013), the top-ranked in TempEval-3 challenge (UzZaman et al., 2013). We refer to this approach as TEE Heidel.

2.2 Filtering (Flt)

We assume that the list of all extracted years gives a probability mass function. We first filter outliers out from it using the Median Absolute Deviation (Hampel, 1974; Leys et al., 2013) with a parameter (γ) that controls the size of the acceptance region for the outlier filter. This parameter is particularly important to filter out present and future references, invariably present in encyclopaedic descriptions. For example, in the sentence "Volta also studied what we now call electrical capacitance", the word *now* would be resolved to '2014' by temporal expression extraction systems, but it should be discarded as an outlier when discovering of Volta's temporal footprint.

2.3 Fitting normal distribution (FND)

A normal distribution is then fitted on the filtered probability mass function. Lower and upper bounds for a temporal footprint are predicted according to two supplementary parameters, α and β. More specifically, the α parameter controls the width of the normal distribution by resizing the width of the Gaussian bell. The β parameter controls the displacement (shift) of the normal distribution. For example, in the case of Wikipedia pages about people, typically this parameter has a negative value (e.g. -5 or -10 years) since the early years of life are rarely mentioned in an encyclopaedic description. We compute the upper and lower bounds of a temporal footprint using the formula $(\mu + \beta) \pm \alpha\sigma$.

We experimented with the following settings:

(a) The *TEE RegEx* strategy consists of extracting all possible dates by using the regular expression previously mentioned and by assigning to the lower and upper bound the earliest and the latest extracted year respectively.

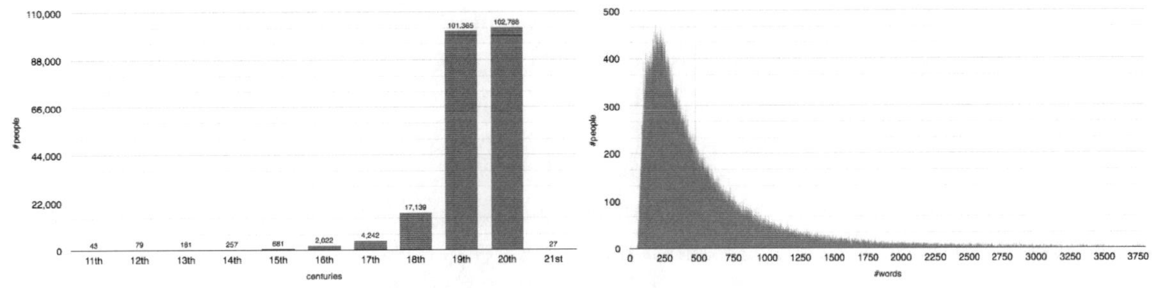

(a) Distribution of Wikipedia pages per century.

(b) Distribution of Wikipedia pages per length (in words).

Figure 2: Exploratory statistics about the test set extracted from DBpedia.

(b) In the *TEE RegEx + Flt* approach, we first discard outliers from the extracted dates and then the earliest and latest dates are used for lower and upper bounds.

(c) For the *TEE RegEx + Flt + FND* strategy, we use the regular expression-based extraction method and then apply filtering and Gaussian fitting.

(d) Finally, for the *TEE Heidel + Flt + FND* setting, we use HeidelTime to extract dates from the associated articles. We than apply filtering and Gaussian fitting.

The parameters α, β and γ are optimised according to a Mean Distance Error (MDE) specifically tailored for temporal intervals (see Appendix A), which intuitively represents the percentage of overlap between the predicted intervals and the gold ones. For each approach we optimised the parameters α, β and γ by using an exhaustive GRID search on a randomly selected subset of 220 people.

3 Data

We applied the methodology on people's Wikipedia pages with the aim of measuring the performance of the proposed approaches. We define a person's temporal footprint as the time between their birth and death. This data has been selected in virtue of the availability of a vast amount of samples along with their curated lower and upper bounds, which are available through DBpedia (Auer et al., 2007). DBpedia was used to obtain a list of Wikipedia web pages about people born since 1000 AD along with their birth and death dates[1]. We checked the consistency of dates using some simple heuristics (the death date does not precede the birth date, a person age cannot be greater than 120 years) and discarded the incongruous entries. We collected 228,824 people who lived from 1000 to 2014. The Figure 2a shows the distribution of people according to the centuries, by considering people belonging to a particular century if they were born in it.

As input to our method, we used associated web pages with some sections discarded, typically containing temporal references invariably pointing to the present, such as *External links*, *See also*, *Citations*, *Footnotes*, *Notes*, *References*, *Further reading*, *Sources*, *Contents* and *Bibliography*. The majority of pages contains from 100 to 500 words (see Figure 2b).

4 Results

Figure 3 depicts the application of the proposed method to the Galileo Galilei's Wikipedia article. The aggregated results with respect to the MDE are showed in Table 1. The TEE Reg + Flt setting outperforms the other approaches. Still, the approaches that use the Gaussian fitting have lower standard deviation.

These results in Table 1 do not take into account the unbalance in the data due to the length of pages (the aggregate numbers are heavily unbalanced towards short pages i.e. those with less than 500 words, as depicted in Figure 2b). We therefore analysed the results with respect to the page length (see Figure 4). TEE RegEx method's performance is negatively affected by the length of the articles. The longer

[1]We used the data set `Persondata` and `Links-To-Wikipedia-Article` from DBpedia 3.9 (`http://wiki.dbpedia.org/Downloads39`)

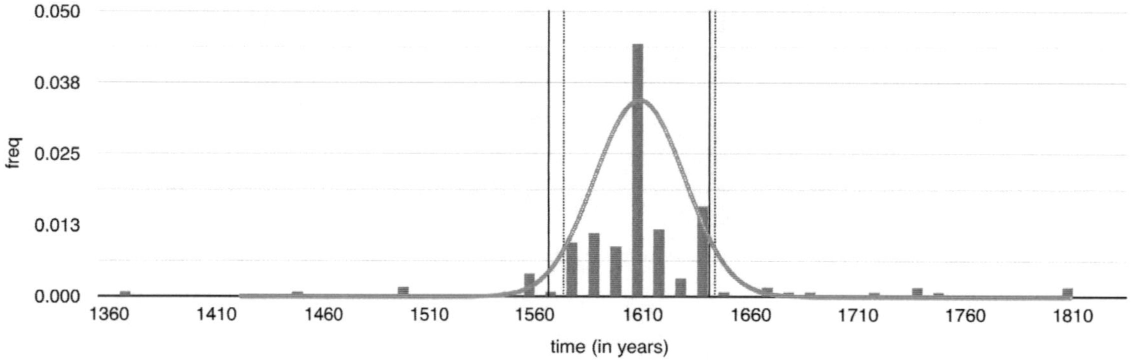

Figure 3: Graphical representation of the output on Galileo Galilei's Wikipedia page. Vertical continuous lines represent the prediction of temporal footprint boundaries, whereas dotted lines represent the real date of birth and death of the Italian scientist. The histogram shows the frequency of mentions of particular years in Galilei's Wikipedia page. The Gaussian bell is plotted in light grey.

Strategy	Mean Distance Error	Standard Deviation
TEE RegEx	0.2636	0.3409
TEE RegEx + Flt	**0.2596**	0.3090
TEE RegEx + Flt + FND	0.3503	0.2430
TEE Heidel + Flt + FND	0.5980	0.2470

Table 1: Results of the four proposed approaches.

a Wikipedia page is, the worse the prediction is. This is expected as longer articles are more likely to contain references to the past or future history, whereas in a short article the dates explicitly mentioned are often birth and death only. The use of the filter (*TEE RegEx+Flt*) generally improves the performance. The approaches that use the Gaussian fitting provide better results in case of longer texts. Still, in spite of its simplicity, the particular regular expression used in this experiment proved to be effective on Wikipedia pages and consequently an exceptionally difficult baseline to beat. Although counter-intuitive, *TEE RegEx + Flt + FND* performs slightly better than the HeidelTime-based method, suggesting that complex temporal information extraction systems do not bring much of useful mentions. This is in part due to the English Wikipedia's Manual of Style[2] which explicitly discourages authors from using implicit temporal expressions (e.g. *now*, *soon*, *currently*, *three years later*) or abbreviations (e.g. *'90*, *eighties* or *17th century*). Due to this bias, we expect a more positive contribution from using a temporal expression extraction system, when the methodology is applied on texts written without style constraints.

5 Conclusions

In this paper we introduced a method to extract temporal footprints of concepts based on mining their textual encyclopaedic description. The proposed methodology uses temporal expression extraction techniques, outlier filtering and Gaussian fitting. Our evaluation on people in Wikipedia showed encouraging results. We found that the use of a sophisticated temporal expression extraction system shows its strength only for long textual descriptions, whereas a simple regular expression-based approach performs better with short texts (the vast majority in Wikipedia pages).

The notion of temporal footprint has not to be interpreted strictly. A more factual interpretation of temporal footprint could be explored, such as temporal projection of a person's impact in history. This would allow to distinguish between people that made important contribution for the future history from those who did not. The predicted interval of Anna Frank's Wikipedia page is an

[2]http://en.wikipedia.org/wiki/Wikipedia:Manual_of_Style_(dates_and_numbers)#Chronological_items

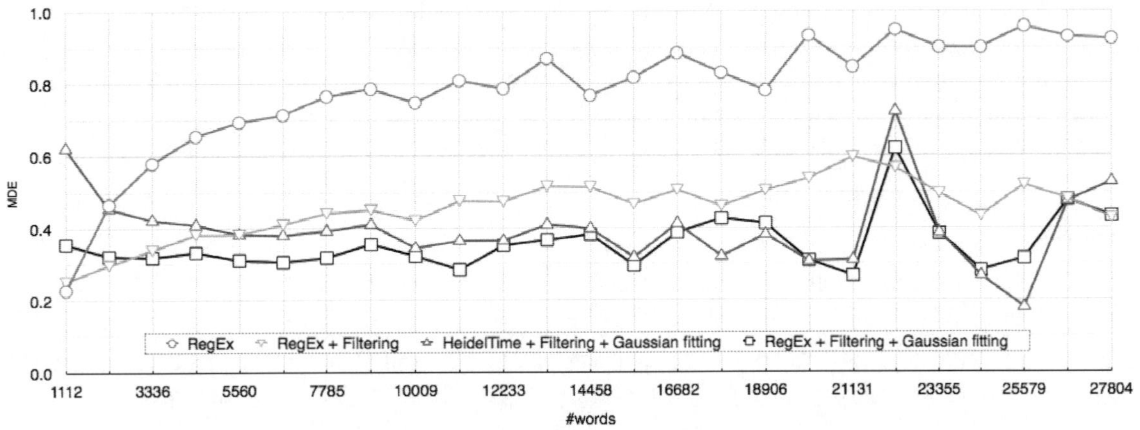

Figure 4: Observed error of the four proposed approaches with respect to the length of Wikipedia pages (the lower the better). Each data point represents the average of each bin. The *TEE RegEx* setting generally provide a very high error which is correlated with the page's length. The use of the outlier filter sensibly improves the performance (*TEE RegEx + Flt*). The approach *TEE RegEx + Flt + FND* is better than *TEE Heidel + Flt + FND* especially with short and medium size pages. The spike near 22000 words is due to a particular small sample.

example of that, and we invite the reader to investigate it via the online demo, which is available at: `http://www.cs.man.ac.uk/~filannim/projects/temporal_footprints/`. This site also provides the data, source code, optimisation details and supplementary graphs to aid the replicability of this work.

Acknowledgements

The authors would like to thank the reviewers for their comments. This paper has greatly benefited from their suggestions and insights. MF would like to acknowledge the support of the UK Engineering and Physical Science Research Council (EPSRC) in the form of doctoral training grant.

Appendix A: Error measure

In interval algebra, the difference between two intervals, $[A]$ and $[B]$, is defined as $[A] - [B] = [A_L - B_U, A_U - B_L]$ (where the subscripts $_L$ and $_U$ indicate lower and upper bound respectively). Unfortunately, this operation is not appropriate to define error measures, because it does not faithfully represent the concept of deviation (Palumbo and Lauro, 2003).

We therefore rely on distances for intervals, which objectively measure the dissimilarity between an observed interval and its forecast (Arroyo and Maté, 2006). In particular, we used De Carvalho's distance (De Carvalho, 1996):

$$d_{DC}([A],[B]) = \frac{d_{IY}^{\lambda}([A],[B])}{w([A] \cup [B])},$$

where $w([A] \cup [B])$ denotes the width of the union interval, and $d_{IY}^{\lambda}([A],[B])$ denotes the Ichino-Yaguchi's distance defined as follows:

$$d_{IY}^{\lambda}([A],[B]) = w([A] \cup [B]) - w([A] \cap [B]) + \lambda(2w([A] \cap [B]) - w([A]) - w([B])).$$

The Mean Distance Error (MDE) based on De Carvalho's distance is defined by:

$$MDE = \frac{1}{n}\sum_{t=1}^{n} \frac{d_{IY}^{\lambda=0}([A_t],[B_t])}{w([A_t] \cup [B_t])} = \frac{1}{n}\sum_{t=1}^{n} \frac{w([A_t] \cup [B_t]) - w([A_t] \cap [B_t])}{w([A_t] \cup [B_t])},$$

where n is the number of total samples. We set $\lambda = 0$ because we do not want to control the effects of the inner-side nearness and the outer-side nearness between the intervals.

The absence of any intersection between the intervals leads to the maximum error, regardless to the distance between the two intervals. A predicted interval far from the gold one has the same error of a predicted interval very close to the gold one, if they both not even minimally overlap with it.

References

Javier Arroyo and Carlos Maté. 2006. Introducing interval time series: Accuracy measures. *COMPSTAT 2006, proceedings in computational statistics*, pages 1139–1146.

Sören Auer, Christian Bizer, Georgi Kobilarov, Jens Lehmann, Richard Cyganiak, and Zachary Ives. 2007. DBpedia: A nucleus for a web of open data. In *The semantic web*, pages 722–735. Springer.

Steven Bethard. 2013. ClearTK-TimeML: A minimalist approach to TempEval 2013. In *Second Joint Conference on Lexical and Computational Semantics (*SEM), Volume 2: Proceedings of the Seventh International Workshop on Semantic Evaluation (SemEval 2013)*, volume 2, pages 10–14, Atlanta, Georgia, USA, June. Association for Computational Linguistics, Association for Computational Linguistics.

Fatima De Carvalho. 1996. Histogrammes et indices de proximité en analyse données symboliques. *Acyes de l'école d'été sur l'analyse des données symboliques. LISE-CEREMADE, Université de Paris IX Dauphine*, pages 101–127.

Oren Etzioni, Michele Banko, Stephen Soderland, and Daniel S. Weld. 2008. Open information extraction from the web. *Commun. ACM*, 51(12):68–74, December.

Michele Filannino, Gavin Brown, and Goran Nenadic. 2013. ManTIME: Temporal expression identification and normalization in the TempEval-3 challenge. In *Second Joint Conference on Lexical and Computational Semantics (*SEM), Volume 2: Proceedings of the Seventh International Workshop on Semantic Evaluation (SemEval 2013)*, pages 53–57, Atlanta, Georgia, USA, June. Association for Computational Linguistics.

Frank R Hampel. 1974. The influence curve and its role in robust estimation. *Journal of the American Statistical Association*, 69(346):383–393.

Heng Ji and Ralph Grishman. 2011. Knowledge base population: Successful approaches and challenges. In *Proceedings of the 49th Annual Meeting of the Association for Computational Linguistics: Human Language Technologies - Volume 1*, HLT '11, pages 1148–1158, Stroudsburg, PA, USA. Association for Computational Linguistics.

Immanuel Kant, Paul Guyer, and Allen W Wood. 1998. *Critique of pure reason*. Cambridge University Press.

Erdal Kuzey and Gerhard Weikum. 2012. Extraction of temporal facts and events from Wikipedia. In *Proceedings of the 2nd Temporal Web Analytics Workshop*, pages 25–32. ACM.

Christophe Leys, Christophe Ley, Olivier Klein, Philippe Bernard, and Laurent Licata. 2013. Detecting outliers: Do not use standard deviation around the mean, use absolute deviation around the median. *Journal of Experimental Social Psychology*, 49(4):764 – 766.

Hector Llorens, Estela Saquete, and Borja Navarro. 2010. TIPSem (english and spanish): Evaluating CRFs and semantic roles in TempEval-2. In *Proceedings of the 5th International Workshop on Semantic Evaluation*, pages 284–291, Uppsala, Sweden, July. Association for Computational Linguistics.

Dat PT Nguyen, Yutaka Matsuo, and Mitsuru Ishizuka. 2007. Relation extraction from wikipedia using subtree mining. In *Proceedings of the National Conference on Artificial Intelligence*, volume 22, page 1414. Menlo Park, CA; Cambridge, MA; London; AAAI Press; MIT Press; 1999.

Francesco Palumbo and CarloN. Lauro. 2003. A PCA for interval-valued data based on midpoints and radii. In H. Yanai, A. Okada, K. Shigemasu, Y. Kano, and J.J. Meulman, editors, *New Developments in Psychometrics*, pages 641–648. Springer Japan.

Anisa Rula, Matteo Palmonari, Axel-Cyrille Ngonga Ngomo, Daniel Gerber, Jens Lehmann, and Lorenz Bühmann. 2014. Hybrid acquisition of temporal scopes for rdf data. In *Proc. of the Extended Semantic Web Conference 2014*.

Jannik Strötgen, Julian Zell, and Michael Gertz. 2013. HeidelTime: Tuning english and developing spanish resources for tempeval-3. In *Second Joint Conference on Lexical and Computational Semantics (*SEM), Volume 2: Proceedings of the Seventh International Workshop on Semantic Evaluation (SemEval 2013)*, pages 15–19, Atlanta, Georgia, USA, June. Association for Computational Linguistics.

Partha Pratim Talukdar, Derry Wijaya, and Tom Mitchell. 2012. Coupled temporal scoping of relational facts. In *Proceedings of the Fifth ACM International Conference on Web Search and Data Mining*, WSDM '12, pages 73–82, New York, NY, USA. ACM.

Naushad UzZaman and James F. Allen. 2010. Event and temporal expression extraction from raw text: First step towards a temporally aware system. *International Journal of Semantic Computing*, 4(4):487–508.

Naushad UzZaman, Hector Llorens, Leon Derczynski, James Allen, Marc Verhagen, and James Pustejovsky. 2013. SemEval-2013 Task 1: TempEval-3: Evaluating time expressions, events, and temporal relations. In *Second Joint Conference on Lexical and Computational Semantics (*SEM), Volume 2: Proceedings of the Seventh International Workshop on Semantic Evaluation (SemEval 2013)*, pages 1–9, Atlanta, Georgia, USA, June. Association for Computational Linguistics.

Marc Verhagen, Robert Gaizauskas, Frank Schilder, Mark Hepple, Graham Katz, and James Pustejovsky. 2007. SemEval-2007 Task 15: TempEval temporal relation identification. In *Proceedings of the 4th International Workshop on Semantic Evaluations*, pages 75–80, Prague.

Marc Verhagen, Roser Saurí, Tommaso Caselli, and James Pustejovsky. 2010. SemEval-2010 Task 13: TempEval-2. In *Proceedings of the 5th International Workshop on Semantic Evaluation*, SemEval '10, pages 57–62, Stroudsburg, PA, USA. Association for Computational Linguistics.

Fei Wu, Raphael Hoffmann, and Daniel S. Weld. 2008. Information extraction from Wikipedia: Moving down the long tail. In *Proceedings of the 14th ACM SIGKDD International Conference on Knowledge Discovery and Data Mining*, KDD '08, pages 731–739, New York, NY, USA. ACM.

Automatic Detection and Analysis of Impressive Japanese Sentences Using Supervised Machine Learning

Daiki Hazure, Masaki Murata, Masato Tokuhisa
Department of Information and Electronics
Tottori University
4-101 Koyama-Minami, Tottori 680-8552, Japan
{s082042,murata,tokuhisa}@ike.tottori-u.ac.jp

Abstract

It is important to write sentences that impress the listener or reader ("impressive sentences") in many cases, such as when drafting political speeches. The study reported here provides useful information for writing such sentences in Japanese. Impressive sentences in Japanese are collected and examined for characteristic words. A number of such words are identified that often appear in impressive sentences, including *jinsei* (human life), *hitobito* (people), *koufuku* (happiness), *yujou* (friendliness), *seishun* (youth), and *ren'ai* (love). Sentences using these words are likely to impress the listener or reader. Machine learning (SVM) is also used to automatically extract impressive sentences. It is found that the use of machine learning enables impressive sentences to be extracted from a large amount of Web documents with higher precision than that obtained with a baseline method, which extracts all sentences as impressive sentences.

1 Introduction

People are always willing to be impressed, and the things that most impress them are liable to be things they need to live, such as food. On the other hand, the wisdom of human beings is recorded in writing, saved in the form of sentences, and inherited by future generations. In this study, we therefore focused on "impressions" and "sentences" and studied sentences that tend to impress the listener or reader. Hereafter for brevity we will refer to these as "impressive sentences". There were two main topics in this study: collecting impressive sentences and analyzing them.

1. Collecting impressive sentences

   We manually collect impressive sentences as well as sentences that are not particularly impressive. By using these sentences and supervised machine learning, we collect more impressive sentences from the Web.

2. Analyzing impressive sentences

   We examine and analyze the impressive sentences. By identifying and collecting words that were often used in them, we clarify the linguistic characteristics of the sentences.

The focus of our study is Japanese sentences.

The study we report in this paper provides useful information for constructing a system that supports the writing of impressive sentences. Such a system would be useful for writing drafts of politicians' speeches or for writing project plan documents where the use of impressive sentences would make the documents more likely to be accepted. In this study, we use natural language processing in an attempt to support persons in their efforts to write impressive sentences.

The main points of the study are as follows:

- This study is the first attempt to use natural language processing for automatic collection and analysis of impressive sentences.

- By collecting sentences automatically and examining the collected data, we identified *jinsei* (human life), *hitobito* (people), *koufuku* (happiness), *yujou* (friendliness), *seishun* (youth), *ren'ai* (love), etc. as words that often appear in impressive sentences. Sentences containing one or more of these words are likely to be impressive sentences. These results should prove to be useful for generating impressive sentences.

- We used machine learning to obtain impressive sentences from a large amount of Web documents at a 0.4 precision rate. This is much higher than the 0.07 rate obtained with a baseline method.

2 Collecting impressive sentences

We first use the Google search engine to collect impressive sentences and sentences that are not particularly impressive. We then use these sentences as supervised data with machine learning to collect more impressive and non-impressive sentences from Web documents.[1]

Hereafter, we will refer to impressive sentences as *positive examples* and non-impressive sentences as *negative examples*.

2.1 Manual collection of impressive sentences

We extract sentences that are obtained by using retrieval words like "... *toiu kotoba ni kando shita*" (I was impressed by the words...) as positive example candidates. We extract sentences that are obtained by using retrieval words like "... *toiu bun*" (the sentences...) as negative example candidates.

Example sentences containing "... *toiu kotoba ni kando shita*" and "... *toiu bun*" are shown below.

Example sentences containing "... *toiu kotoba ni kando shita*":

"*mainichi ga*	*mirai*"	*toiu*	*kotoba ni*	*kando-shita.*
(every day)	(future)	(of)	(word)	(was impressed)

(I was impressed by the words "Every day is the future.")

Example sentences containing "... *toiu bun*":

kanojo wa	*supoutsu wo*	*suru noga*	*suki desu*	*toiu*	*bun*
(she)	(sport)	(play)	(like)	(of)	(sentence)

(The sentence "She likes playing sports")

In the above examples, the sentences *mainichi ga mirai* (Every day is the future) and *michi wa hito to hito no kakehashi desu* (A road is a bridge connecting people with other people) are used as positive example candidates. The sentences *yomitori senyou* (Read only) and *kanojo wa supoutsu wo suru noga suki desu* (She likes playing sports) are used as negative example candidates.

We also use the Google search engine to retrieve famous sentences and use them as positive example candidates.[2] We collect sentences from sources such as Yahoo! News and use them as negative example candidates.

We manually judge whether candidates are positive and negative, and in so doing obtain accurate positive and negative examples.

Our judgment criterion is that sentences that received the comment "*kando shita*" (was impressed by) and famous sentences are judged to be positive. Sentences that do not have emphatic punctuation such as exclamation marks or that describe objective facts only are judged to be negative.

We performed the above procedure and obtained 1,018 positive examples and 406 negative examples.

2.2 Using supervised machine learning to collect impressive sentences

We conduct machine learning using the positive and negative examples obtained as described in Section 2.1 as supervised data. We use sentences in Web documents as inputs for machine learning. Machine learning is used to judge whether the sentences are impressive. In this way we collect impressive sentences from Web documents.

The specific procedure is as follows:

[1] We used the Web documents that Kawahara et al. collected (Kawahara and Kurohashi, 2006).

[2] Some famous sentences are obtained from http://www.meigensyu.com/.

Table 1: Words with high appearance probabilities in positive examples

Word	Ratio of positive	Freq. of positive	Freq. of negative	Word	Ratio of positive	Freq. of positive	Freq. of negative
koufuku (happiness)	1.00	83	0	*aisuru* (love)	0.94	30	2
yujou (friendliness)	1.00	29	0	*arayuru* (every)	0.93	14	1
seishun (youth)	1.00	18	0	*omae* (you)	0.93	13	1
kanashimi (sadness)	1.00	12	0	*shunkan* (moment)	0.92	11	1
sonzai (existence)	1.00	10	0	*jinsei* (life)	0.91	145	14
...	...	...	...	*mirai* (future)	0.91	20	2
wareware (we)	0.97	37	1	*shiawase* (happiness)	0.91	20	2
fukou (unhappiness)	0.97	32	1	*yorokobi* (delight)	0.91	10	1
aisa (love)	0.96	23	1	*onna* (woman)	0.91	115	12
ren'ai (love)	0.96	44	2	*unmei* (destiny)	0.90	19	2
koi (love)	0.95	122	7	*shinu* (die)	0.90	37	4
kodoku (loneliness)	0.94	32	2	...	...	...	...
konoyo (this world)	0.94	16	1	*hitobito* (people)	0.81	17	4
aishi (love)	0.94	31	2	*kandou* (impression)	0.80	8	2

1. The 1,018 positive and 406 negative examples obtained as described in Section 2.1 are used as supervised data.

2. We use the supervised data to conduct machine learning. The machine learning is used to judge whether 10,000 sentences newly obtained from Web documents are positive or negative. We manually check sentences judged to be positive and construct new positive and negative examples. We add the new examples to the supervised data.

3. We repeat the above step 2 procedure ten times.

We use a support vector machine (SVM) for machine learning (Cristianini and Shawe-Taylor, 2000; Kudoh and Matsumoto, 2000; Isozaki and Kazawa, 2002; Murata et al., 2002; Takeuchi and Collier, 2003; Mitsumori et al., 2005; Chen and Wen, 2006; Murata et al., 2011).[3] We use unigram words whose parts of speech (POSs) are nouns, verbs, adjectives, adjectival verbs, adnominals, and interjections as features used in machine learning.

The judgment criteria for positive and negative examples in this section are as follows: Sentences for which a judge can spontaneously produce certain comments are judged to be positive examples. Sentences that describe objective facts only are judged to be negative examples.

We repeated the procedure ten times. In total, 275 positive and 3,006 negative examples were obtained. When we add these examples to the original ones, the totals become 1,293 positive and 3,412 negative examples. In this case we repeated the learning procedure ten times, but more positive and negative examples could be obtained by repeating it more than ten times.

A subject (Subject A) judged whether the examples were positive or negative. Three other subjects evaluated 20 examples that were judged positive and 20 that were judged negative by Subject A. We compared Subject A's judgments and the majority voting results of the other three subjects' judgments and obtained 0.58 (moderate agreement) as a kappa value.

3 Analysis of collected impressive sentences

In our analysis, we used the abovementioned 1,293 positive and 3,412 negative examples. We used certain words to examine the impressive sentences.

We extracted a number of words from the positive and negative examples. For each word, we calculated its appearance frequency in positive and negative examples and the ratio of its frequency in positive examples to its frequency in negative ones. We extracted words for which the ratio was higher than 0.8 and words that were at least four times likelier to appear in positive examples than in negative ones. Some of the extracted words are shown in Table 1. In the table, "Ratio appearing in positive" indicates the ratio

[3]In this study, we use a quadratic polynomial kernel as a kernel function of SVM. We confirmed that the kernel produced good performance in preliminary experiments.

Table 2: Impressive sentence extraction performance of various methods

Method	Precision	Recall	F measure
ML method (0th)	0.06	0.25	0.10
ML method (first)	0.26	0.08	0.12
ML method (second)	0.29	0.07	0.11
ML method (fifth)	0.31	0.05	0.09
ML method (10th)	0.40	0.05	0.09
Baseline method	0.07	1.00	0.12
Pattern method 1	0.11	0.08	0.09
Pattern method 2	1.00	0.002	0.003

of the word's frequency in positive examples to its frequency in the data. "Frequency in positive" and "Frequency in negative" respectively show the number of times the word appears in positive and negative examples.

As the table shows, the words obtaining the highest ratios included *jinsei* (human life), *hitobito* (people), *koufuku* (happiness), *yujou* (friendliness), *seishun* (youth), and *ren'ai* (love). Sentences in which one or more of these words are used are likely to be impressive sentences.

These results are the most important and interesting points in this paper. We found that using the words shown in the table is a good approach to use if we would like to generate impressive sentences.

Shown below are example sentences containing *jinsei* (human life), *hitobito* (people), and *koufuku* (happiness).

Example sentences containing *jinsei* (life):

jinsei wa	*douro no*	*youna mono da.*	*ichibanno*	*chikamichi wa*	*taitei*	*ichiban warui.*	*michi da.*
(life)	(road)	(be like)	(first)	(shortcut)	(usually)	(worst)	(road)

(Life is like a road. The first shortcut is usually the worst road.)

Example sentences containing *hitobito* (people):

hitobito wa	*kanashimi wo*	*wakachi attekureru*	*tomodachi*	*sae ireba*	*kanashimi wo*	*yawaragerareru.*
(people)	(sadness)	(share)	(friend)	(if only they have)	(sadness)	(can soften)

(People can soften their sadness, if only they have a friend with whom they can share it.)

Example sentences containing *koufuku* (happiness):

fukouna	*hito wa*	*kibou wo*	*mote.*	*koufukuna*	*hito wa*	*youjin seyo.*
(unhappy)	(person)	(hope)	(should have)	(happy)	(person)	(should be on one's guard)

(Unhappy people should have hope. Happy people should be on their guard.)

4 Automatic impressive sentence extraction performance

The method we describe in this paper is a useful one for automatically extracting impressive sentences. In this section, we evaluate the extraction performance of this and other methods.

The evaluation results are shown in Table 2. The data set for evaluation consists of 10,000 new sentences from Web documents. We use each method to extract positive sentences from the set for evaluation. We then randomly extract 100 data items (200 for the baseline method only) from the sentences extracted by each method and manually evaluate them. From the evaluation results we approximately calculate the precision rates, the recall rates, and the F-measures.

We estimate the denominator of the recall rate from the number of positive examples detected by the baseline method. The baseline method judges that all the inputs are positive.

In the "ML method (xth)" we use supervised data for machine learning after adding the xth positive and negative examples to the supervised data (by the method in Section 2.2). In "Pattern method 1" we extract sentences that contain words whose positive appearance ratio is at least 0.8 and that appear at least four times as positive examples. In "Pattern method 2" we extract sentences that contain the word "*kando*" (impression) as positive examples.

With machine learning we obtain a precision rate of 0.40 after we add the 10th positive and negative examples to the supervised data. This precision rate is much higher than the 0.07 rate we obtain with the baseline method.

Some may think that the 0.40 precision rate obtained with machine learning is low. However, since the task of extracting impressive sentences is a very difficult one, and since the rate is much higher than the baseline method rate, we can say that the machine learning results are at least adequate.

5 Related studies

Many methods have been reported that estimated the orientation (positive or negative contents) or the emotion of a sentence (Turney and Littman, 2003; Pang and Lee, 2008; Kim and Hovy, 2004; Alm et al., 2005; Aman and Szpakowicz, 2007; Strapparava and Mihalcea, 2008; Inkpen et al., 2009; Neviarouskaya et al., 2009). However, the studies did not address the task of collecting and analyzing impressive sentences to support the generation of such sentences.

There have been studies that addressed the task of automatically evaluating sentences to support sentence generation (Bangalore and Whittaker, 2000; Mutton and Dale, 2007). However, the studies did not address the task of generating impressive sentences.

In our study, we used machine learning to extract impressive sentences. There have been other studies as well in which machine learning was used to extract information (Murata et al., 2011; Stijn De Saeger and Hashimoto, 2009). Murata et al. extracted articles describing problems, their solutions, and their causes (Murata et al., 2011). Saeger et al. extracted several types of words from a large scale of Web documents by using machine learning (Stijn De Saeger and Hashimoto, 2009). In their method, they manually make supervised data sets for extracted words and extract more words from Web documents using supervised methods. Their study is similar to ours in that both use the same framework of manually making a small scale supervised data set and then extracting more data items from Web documents.

6 Conclusion

We collected sentences in Japanese that impressed readers ("impressive sentences") and examined them through the use of characteristic words in order to support the generation of impressive sentences. In our examination, we obtained *jinsei* (human life), *hitobito* (people), *koufuku* (happiness), *yujou* (friendliness), *seishun* (youth), *ren'ai* (love), etc. as words that often appear in impressive sentences. Sentences in which one or more of these words are used would be likely to impress the listener or reader. The results we obtained should provide useful information for generating impressive sentences.

In this study, we used machine learning to extract impressive sentences and found that with this method we could extract them from a large amount of Web documents with a precision rate of 0.40.

In future work, we intend to use this method to collect more impressive sentences. We also plan to analyze the sentences by using not only words but also parameters such as syntax patterns and rhetorical expressions.

Acknowledgment

This work was supported by JSPS KAKENHI Grant Number 23500178.

References

Cecilia O. Alm, Dan Roth, and Richard Sproat. 2005. Emotions from text: Machine learning for text-based emotion prediction. In *Proceedings of Human Language Technology Conference and Conference on Empirical Methods in Natural Language (HLT/EMNLP 2005)*, pages 579–586.

Saima Aman and Stan Szpakowicz. 2007. Identifying expressions of emotion in text. In *Proceedings of the 10th International Conference on Text, Speech and Dialogue (TSD'07)*, pages 196–205.

Srinivas Bangalore and Owen Rambow and Steve Whittaker. 2000. Evaluation metrics for generation. In *Proceedings of the first international conference on Natural language generation (INLG '00)*, pages 1–8.

Peng Chen and Tao Wen. 2006. Margin maximization model of text classification based on support vector machines. In *Machine Learning and Cybernetics*, pages 3514–3518.

Nello Cristianini and John Shawe-Taylor. 2000. *An introduction to support vector machines and other kernel-based learning methods*. Cambridge University Press.

Diana Inkpen, Fazel Keshtkar, and Diman Ghazi. 2009. Analysis and generation of emotion in texts. In *Knowledge Engineering: Principle and Technique, KEPT 2009*, pages 3–14.

Hideki Isozaki and Hideto Kazawa. 2002. Efficient support vector classifiers for named entity recognition. *Proceedings of the 19th International Conference on Computational Linguistics (COLING-2002)*, pages 1–7.

Daisuke Kawahara and Sadao Kurohashi. 2006. Case frame compilation from the web using high-performance computing. *Proceedings of the 5th International Conference on Language Resources and Evaluation,*, pages 1–4.

Soo-Min Kim and Eduard Hovy. 2004. Determining the sentiment of opinions. In *Proceedings of Coling 2004*, pages 1367–1373.

Taku Kudoh and Yuji Matsumoto. 2000. Use of support vector learning for chunk identification. *CoNLL-2000*, pages 142–144.

Tomohiro Mitsumori, Sevrani Fation, Masaki Murata, Kouichi Doi, and Hirohumi Doi. 2005. Gene/protein name recognition based on support vector machine using dictionary as features. *BMC Bioinformatics*, 6(Suppl 1)(S8):1–10.

Masaki Murata, Qing Ma, and Hitoshi Isahara. 2002. Comparison of three machine-learning methods for Thai part-of-speech tagging. *ACM Transactions on Asian Language Information Processing*, 1(2):145–158.

Masaki Murata, Hiroki Tanji, Kazuhide Yamamoto, Stijn De Saeger, Yasunori Kakizawa, and Kentaro Torisawa. 2011. Extraction from the web of articles describing problems, their solutions, and their causes. *IEICE Transactions on Information and Systems*, E94–D(3):734–737.

Andrew Mutton and Mark Dras and Stephen Wan and Robert Dale. 2007. Gleu: Automatic evaluation of sentence-level fluency. In *Proceedings of the 45th Annual Meeting of the Association of Computational Linguistics (ACL 2007)*, pages 344–351.

Alena Neviarouskaya, Helmut Prendinger, and Mitsuru Ishizuka. 2009. Compositionality principle in recognition of fine-grained emotions from text. In *Proceedings of 4th International AAAI Conference on Weblogs and Social Media (ICWSM 2009)*, pages 278–281.

Bo Pang and Lillian Lee. 2008. Opinion minding and sentiment analysis. *Foundation and Trend in Information Retrieval*, 2(1-2):1–135.

Kentaro Torisawa Masaki Murata Ichiro Yamada Kow Kuroda Stijn De Saeger, Jun'ichi Kazama and Chikara Hashimoto. 2009. A web service for automatic word class acquisition. In *Proceedings of 3rd International Universal Communication Symposium (IUCS 2009)*, pages 132–137.

Carlo Strapparava and Rada Mihalcea. 2008. Learning to identify emotions in text. In *Proceedings of the 2008 ACM Symposium on Applied Computing (SAC '08)*, page 1556?1560.

Koichi Takeuchi and Nigel Collier. 2003. Bio-medical entity extraction using support vector machine. *Proceedings of the ACL 2003 Workshop on NLP in Biomedicine*, pages 57–64.

Peter D. Turney and Michael L. Littman. 2003. Measuring praise and criticism: Inference of semantic orientation from association. *ACM Transactions on Information Systems (TOIS)*, 21(4):315–346.

Proposition Knowledge Graphs

Gabriel Stanovsky **Omer Levy** **Ido Dagan**
Computer Science Department, Bar-Ilan University
{gabriel.satanovsky, omerlevy}@gmail.com
dagan@cs.biu.ac.il

Abstract

Open Information Extraction (Open IE) is a promising approach for unrestricted Information Discovery (ID). While Open IE is a highly scalable approach, allowing unsupervised relation extraction from open domains, it currently has some limitations. First, it lacks the expressiveness needed to properly represent and extract complex assertions that are abundant in text. Second, it does not consolidate the extracted propositions, which causes simple queries above Open IE assertions to return insufficient or redundant information. To address these limitations, we propose in this position paper a novel representation for ID – Propositional Knowledge Graphs (PKG). PKGs extend the Open IE paradigm by representing semantic inter-proposition relations in a traversable graph. We outline an approach for constructing PKGs from single and multiple texts, and highlight a variety of high-level applications that may leverage PKGs as their underlying information discovery and representation framework.

1 Introduction

Information discovery from text (ID) aims to provide a consolidated and explorable data representation of an input document or a collection of documents addressing a common topic. Ideally, this representation would separate the input into logically discrete units, omit redundancies in the original text, and provide semantic relations between the basic units of the representation. This representation can then be used by human readers as a convenient and succinct format, or by subsequent NLP tasks (such as question answering and multidocument summarization) as a structured input representation.

A common approach to ID is to extract propositions conveyed in the text by applying either supervised Information Extraction (IE) techniques (Cowie and Lehnert, 1996), to recover propositions covering a predefined set of relations (Auer et al., 2007; Suchanek et al., 2008), or more recently, *Open* Information Extraction (Open IE) (Etzioni et al., 2008), which discovers open-domain relations (Zhu et al., 2009; Wu et al., 2008). In Open IE, natural language propositions are extracted from text, based on surface or syntactic patterns, and are then represented as predicate-argument tuples, where each element is a natural language string. While Open IE presents a promising direction for ID, thanks to its robustness and scalability across domains, we argue that it currently lacks representation power in two major aspects: **representing complex propositions extracted from discourse**, such as interdependent propositions or implicitly conveyed propositions, and **consolidating propositions extracted across multiple sources**, which leads to either insufficient or redundant information when exploring a set of Open IE extractions.

In this position paper we outline *Propositional Knowledge Graphs* (PKG), a representation which addresses both of Open IE's mentioned drawbacks. The graph's nodes are discrete propositions extracted from text, and edges are drawn where semantic relations between propositions exists. Such relations can be inferred from a single discourse, or from multiple text fragments along with background knowledge – by applying methods such as textual entailment recognition (Dagan et al., 2013) – which consolidates the information within the graph. We discuss this representation as a useful input for semantic applications, and describe work we have been doing towards implementing such a framework.

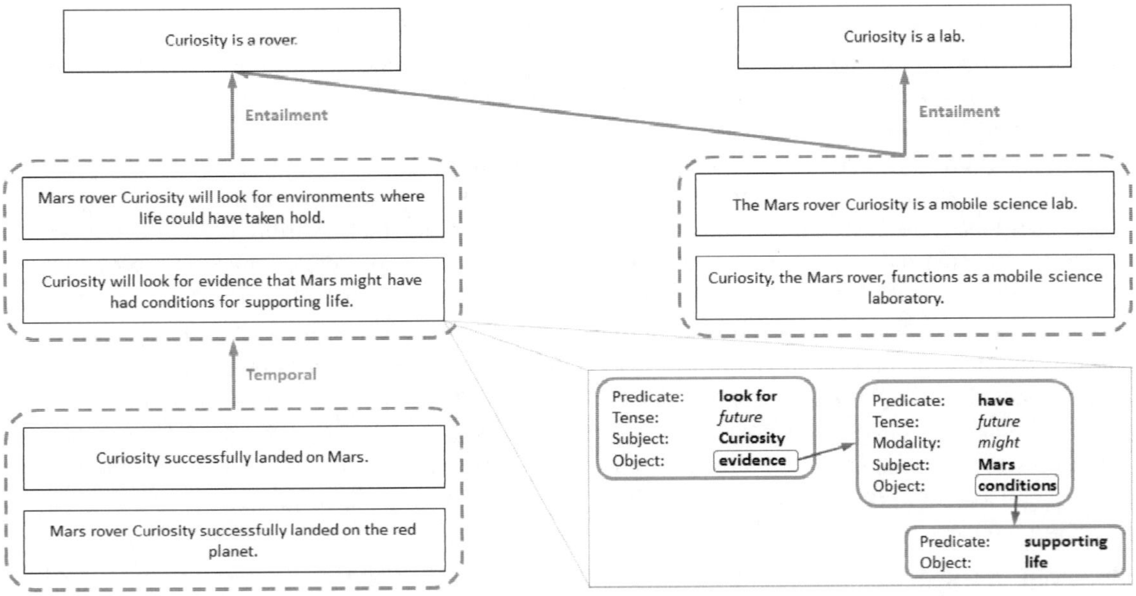

Figure 1: An excerpt from a PKG, containing a few propositions extracted from news reports about Curiosity (the Mars rover) and their relations. The dashed boundaries in the figure denote paraphrase cliques, meaning that all propositions within them are mutually entailing. Some of these propositions are complex, and the bottom-right corner illustrates how one of them can be represented by inter-connected sub-propositions.

2 Approach: Discover Inter-Proposition Relations

We propose a novel approach for textual information discovery and representation that enhances the expressiveness of Open IE with structural power similar to traditional knowledge graphs. Our representation aims to extract all the information conveyed by text to a traversable graph format – a Propositional Knowledge Graph (PKG). The graph's nodes are *natural language propositions* and its labeled edges are *semantic relations* between these propositions. Figure 1 illustrates an excerpt of a PKG.

We separate the construction of such graphs into two phases, each of which addresses one of the aforementioned limitations of current Open IE. The first phase (described in section 2.1) is the extraction of *complex propositions* from a single discourse. This phase extends upon the definition of Open IE extractions to gain a more expressive paradigm and improve the recall of extracted propositions. In this extension, a single assertion is represented by a set of interconnected propositions. An example can be seen in the bottom right of Figure 1. The second phase (described in section 2.2) deals with the *consolidation* of propositions extracted in the first phase. This is done by drawing relations such as *entailment* and *temporal succession* between these propositions, which can be inferred utilizing background knowledge applied on multiple text fragments.

2.1 Relations Implied by Discourse

Current Open IE representation schemes lack the expressibility to represent certain quite common propositions implied by syntax, hindering Open IE's potential as an information discovery framework. We discuss several cases in which this limitation is evident, and describe possible solutions within our proposed framework.

Embedded and Interrelated Propositions Common Open IE systems retrieve only propositions in which both predicates and arguments are instantiated in succession in the surface form. For such propositions, these systems produce *independent* tuples (typically a *(subject, verb, object)* triplet) consisting of a predicate and a list of its arguments, all expressed in natural language, in the same way they originally appeared in the sentence. This methodology lacks the ability to represent cases in which propositions are inherently embedded, such as conditionals and propositional arguments (e.g. "Senator Kennedy asked congress to pass the bill"). Mausam et al. (2012) introduced a *context analysis* layer, extending this representation with an additional field per tuple, which intends to represent the *factuality* of the extraction, accounting specifically for cases of conditionals and attribution. For instance, the assertion "If he wins five key states, Romney will be elected President" will be represented as *((Romney; will be elected; President) ClausalModifier if; he wins five key states)*.

While these methods capture some of the propositions conveyed by text, they fail to retrieve other propositions expressed by more sophisticated syntactic constructs. Consider the sentence from Figure 1 "Curiosity will look for evidence that Mars might have had conditions for supporting life". It exhibits a construction which the independent tuples format seems to fall short from representing. Our proposed representation for this sentence is depicted in the bottom right of Figure 1. We represent the complexity of the sentence through a nested structure of interlinked propositions, each composed of a single predicate and its syntactic arguments and modifiers. In addition, we model certain syntactic variabilities as features, such as tense, negation, passive voice, etc. Thus, a single assertion is represented through the discrete propositions it conveys, along with their inter-relations. In addition to the expressibility that this representation offers, an immediate gain is the often recurring case in which a part of a proposition (for example, one of the arguments) immediately implies another proposition. For instance, "The Mars rover Curiosity is a mobile science lab" implies that "Curiosity is a rover", and does so syntactically.

Implicit propositions Certain propositions which are conveyed by the text are not explicitly expressed in the surface form. Consider, for instance, the sentence "Facebook's acquisition of WhatsApp occurred yesterday". It introduces the proposition *(Facebook, acquired, WhatsApp)* through *nominalization*. Current Open IE formalisms are unable to extract such triplets, since the necessary predicate (namely "acquired") does not appear in the surface form. Implicit propositions might be introduced in many other linguistic constructs, such as: *appositions* ("The company, Random House, doesn't report its earnings." implies that Random House is a company), *adjectives* ("Tall John walked home" implies that John is tall), and *possessives* ("John's book is on the table" implies that John has a book). We intend to syntactically identify these implicit propositions, and make them explicit in our representation.

For further analysis of syntax-driven proposition representation, see our recent work (Stanovsky et al., 2014). We believe that this extension of Open IE representation is feasibly extractable from syntactic parse trees, and are currently working on automatic conversion from Stanford dependencies (de Marneffe and Manning, 2008) to interconnected propositions as described.

2.2 Consolidating Information across Propositions

While Open IE is indeed much more scalable than supervised approaches, it does not consolidate natural language expressions, which leads to either insufficient or redundant information when accessing a repository of Open IE extractions. As an illustrating example, querying the University of Washington's Open IE demo (`openie.cs.washington.edu`) for the generally equivalent *relieves headache* or *treats headache* returns two different lists of entities; out of the top few results, the only answers these queries seem to agree on are *caffeine* and *sex*. Desirably, an information discovery platform should return identical results (or at least very similar ones) to these queries. This is a major drawback relative to supervised knowledge representations, such as Freebase (Bollacker et al., 2008), which map natural language expressions to canonical formal representations (e.g. the *treatments* relation in Freebase).

While much relational information can be salvaged from the original text, many inter-propositional relations stem from background knowledge and our understanding of language. Perhaps the most prominent of these is the *entailment* relation, as demonstrated in Figure 1. We rely on the definition of *textual entailment* as defined by Dagan et al. (2013): proposition T entails proposition H if humans reading T would typically infer that H is most likely true. Entailment provides an effective structure for aggregating natural-language based information; it merges semantically equivalent propositions into cliques, and induces specification-generalization edges between them (if T entails H, then H is more general).

Figure 1 demonstrates the usefulness of entailment in organizing the propositions within a PKG. For example, the two statements describing Curiosity as a mobile science lab (middle right) originated from two different texts. However, in a PKG, they are marked as paraphrases (mutually entailing), and both entail an additional proposition from a third source: "Curiosity is a lab". If one were to query all the propositions that entail "Curiosity is a lab" – e.g. in response to the query "What is Curiosity?" – all three propositions would be retrieved, even though their surface forms may have "functions as" instead of "is" or "laboratory" instead of "lab".

We have recently taken some first steps in this direction, investigating algorithms for constructing entailment edges over sets of related propositions (Levy et al., 2014). Even between simple propositions, recognizing entailment is challenging. We are currently working on new methods that will leverage structured and unstructured data to recognize entailment for Open IE propositions. There are additional relations, besides entailment, that should desirably be represented in PKGs as well. Two such examples are *temporal relations* (depicted in Figure 1) and *causality*. Investigating and adapting methods for recognizing and utilizing these relations is intended for future work.

3 Applications

An appealing application of knowledge graphs is question answering (QA). In this section we demonstrate how our representation may facilitate more sophisticated information access scenarios.

Structured Queries Queries over structured data give the user the power to receive targeted answers for her queries. Consider for example the query "electric cars on sale in Canada". PKGs can give the power of queries over *structured* data to the domain of *unstructured* information. To answer our query, we can search the PKG for all of the propositions that *entail* these two propositions: (1) "X is an electric car", (2) "X is on sale in Canada", where X is a variable. The list of X instantiations is the answer to our structured query. Our knowledge structure enables even more sophisticated queries that involve more than one variable. For example, "Japanese corporations that bought Australian start-ups" retrieves a collection of pairs (X, Y) where X is the Japanese corporation that bought Y, an Australian start-up.

Summarization Multi-document summarization gives the user the ability to compactly assimilate information from multiple documents on the same topic. PKGs can be a natural platform leveraged by summarization because: (1) they would contain the information from those documents as fine-grained propositions (2) they represent the semantic relations between those propositions. These semantic relations can be leveraged to create high-quality summarizations. For example, the paraphrase (mutual entailment) relation prevents redundancy. Links of a temporal or causal nature can also dictate the order in which each proposition is presented. A recent method of summarizing text with entailment graphs (Gupta et al., 2014) demonstrates the appeal and feasibility of this application.

Faceted Search Faceted search allows a user to interactively navigate a PKG. Adler et al. (2012) demonstrate this concept on a limited proposition graph. When searching for "headache" in their demo, the user can drill-down to find possible causes or remedies, and even focus on subcategories of those; for example, finding the foods which relieve headaches. As opposed to the structured query application, retrieval is not fully automated, but rather interactive. It thus allows users to explore and discover new information they might not have considered a-priori.

4 Discussion

In this position paper we outlined a framework for information discovery that leverages and extends Open IE, while addressing two of its current major drawbacks. The proposed framework enriches Open IE by representing natural language in a traversable graph, composed of propositions and their semantic interrelations – A *Propositional Knowledge Graph* (PKG). The resulting structure provides a representation in two levels: locally, at *sentence level*, by representing the syntactic proposition structure embedded in a single sentence, and globally, at *inter-proposition level*, where relations are drawn between propositions from discourse, or from various sources.

At the *sentence level*, PKG can be compared to Abstract Meaning Representation (AMR) (Banarescu et al., 2013), which maps a sentence onto a hierarchical structure of propositions (predicate-argument relations) - a "meaning representation". AMR uses Propbank (Kingsbury and Palmer, 2003) for predicates' meaning representation, where possible, and ungrounded natural language, where no respective

Propbank lexicon entry exists. While AMR relies on a deep semantic interpretation, our sentence level representation is more conservative (and thus, hopefully, more feasible) and can be obtained by syntactic interpretation.

At *inter-proposition level*, PKG can be compared with traditional Knowledge Graphs (such as Freebase and Google's Knowledge Graph). These Knowledge Graphs, in contrast with PKGs, require manual intervention and aim to cover a rich set of relations using formal language and a pre-specified schema, thus many relations are inevitably left out (e.g. the relation *cracked*, as in *(Alan Turing, cracked, the Enigma)* does not exist in Freebase).

We believe that PKGs are a promising extension of Open IE's unsupervised traits, for combining aspects of information representation - on a local scale, providing a rich schema for representing sentences, and on a global scale providing an automated and consolidated method for structuring knowledge.

References

Meni Adler, Jonathan Berant, and Ido Dagan. 2012. Entailment-based text exploration with application to the health-care domain. In *Proceedings of the System Demonstrations of the 50th Annual Meeting of the Association for Computational Linguistics (ACL 2012)*, pages 79–84.

Sören Auer, Christian Bizer, Georgi Kobilarov, Jens Lehmann, Richard Cyganiak, and Zachary Ives. 2007. Dbpedia: A nucleus for a web of open data. In *The semantic web*, pages 722–735. Springer.

Laura Banarescu, Claire Bonial, Shu Cai, Madalina Georgescu, Kira Griffitt, Ulf Hermjakob, Kevin Knight, Philipp Koehn, Martha Palmer, and Nathan Schneider. 2013. Abstract meaning representation for sembanking.

Kurt Bollacker, Colin Evans, Praveen Paritosh, Tim Sturge, and Jamie Taylor. 2008. Freebase: a collaboratively created graph database for structuring human knowledge. In *Proceedings of the 2008 ACM SIGMOD international conference on Management of data*, pages 1247–1250. ACM.

Jim Cowie and Wendy Lehnert. 1996. Information extraction. *Communications of the ACM*, 39(1):80–91.

Ido Dagan, Dan Roth, Mark Sammons, and Fabio Massimo Zanzotto. 2013. Recognizing textual entailment: Models and applications. *Synthesis Lectures on Human Language Technologies*, 6(4):1–220.

Marie-Catherine de Marneffe and Christopher D. Manning. 2008. The Stanford typed dependencies representation. In *Coling 2008: Proceedings of the workshop on Cross-Framework and Cross-Domain Parser Evaluation*, pages 1–8, Manchester, UK, August. Coling 2008 Organizing Committee.

Oren Etzioni, Michele Banko, Stephen Soderland, and Daniel S Weld. 2008. Open information extraction from the Web. *Communications of the ACM*, 51(12):68–74.

Anand Gupta, Manpreet Kathuria, Shachar Mirkin, Adarsh Singh, and Aseem Goyal. 2014. Text summarization through entailment-based minimum vertex cover. In **SEM*.

Paul Kingsbury and Martha Palmer. 2003. Propbank: the next level of treebank. In *Proceedings of Treebanks and lexical Theories*, volume 3.

Omer Levy, Ido Dagan, and Jacob Goldberger. 2014. Focused entailment graphs for open ie propositions. In *Proceedings of the Eighteenth Conference on Computational Natural Language Learning*, Baltimore, Maryland, USA, June. Association for Computational Linguistics.

Mausam, Michael Schmitz, Stephen Soderland, Robert Bart, and Oren Etzioni. 2012. Open language learning for information extraction. In *Proceedings of the 2012 Joint Conference on Empirical Methods in Natural Language Processing and Computational Natural Language Learning*, pages 523–534, Jeju Island, Korea, July. Association for Computational Linguistics.

Gabriel Stanovsky, Jessica Ficler, Ido Dagan, and Yoav Goldberg. 2014. Intermediary semantic representation through proposition structures. In *Workshop on Semantic Parsing*, Baltimore, Maryland, USA, June. Association for Computational Linguistics.

Fabian M Suchanek, Gjergji Kasneci, and Gerhard Weikum. 2008. Yago: A large ontology from wikipedia and wordnet. *Web Semantics: Science, Services and Agents on the World Wide Web*, 6(3):203–217.

Fei Wu, Raphael Hoffmann, and Daniel S Weld. 2008. Information extraction from wikipedia: Moving down the long tail. In *Proceedings of the 14th ACM SIGKDD international conference on Knowledge discovery and data mining*, pages 731–739. ACM.

Jun Zhu, Zaiqing Nie, Xiaojiang Liu, Bo Zhang, and Ji-Rong Wen. 2009. Statsnowball: a statistical approach to extracting entity relationships. In *Proceedings of the 18th international conference on World wide web*, pages 101–110. ACM.

Using Distributional Semantics to Trace Influence and Imitation in Romantic Orientalist Poetry

Nitish Aggarwal
Insight Centre for Data Analytics
National University of Ireland
Galway, Ireland
nitish.aggarwal@deri.org

Justin Tonra
School of Humanities
National University of Ireland
Galway, Ireland
justin.tonra@nuigalway.ie

Paul Buitelaar
Insight Centre for Data Analytics
National University of Ireland
Galway, Ireland
paul.buitelaar@deri.org

Abstract

In this paper, we investigate whether textual analysis can yield evidence of shared vocabulary or formal textual characteristics in the works of 19th century poets Lord Byron and Thomas Moore in the genre of Romantic Orientalism. In particular, we identify and trace Byron's influence on Moore's writings to query whether Moore imitated Byron, as many reviewers of the time suggested. We use a Distributional Semantic Model (DSM) to analyze if there is a shared vocabulary of Romantic Orientalism, or if it is possible to characterize a literary genre in terms of vocabulary, rather than in terms of the particular plots, characters and themes. We discuss the results that DSM models are able to provide for an abstract overview of the influence of Lord Byron's work on Thomas Moore.

1 Introduction

Literary criticism has often marshalled the serendipitous discovery in the service of constructing an argument or a critical judgment. Such serendipity can take material or cognitive form, and provide the raw materials for analysis and conjecture. In literary criticism, arguments are often based upon evidence gleaned from close reading of a text in support of a hypothesis, but quantitative methods have shown how literary texts can yield evidence that is not immediately discernible to the human eye for a similar interpretive purposes. In literary studies, computers have assisted in the collection of such data with varying degrees of complexity and sophistication for about half a century. How can we use the information from such computing processes for creating new knowledge, or, in literary-critical terms, for articulating the meaning in a text? To what degree can literary criticism and computing enrich one another? Is algorithmic criticism derived from algorithmic manipulation of text (Ramsay, 2011) possible?

Inspired by general questions such as these, this paper discusses a particular project that uses Distributional Semantics to trace influence and imitation between two particular poets writing in the genre of Romantic Orientalism. Our intuition is that if text analysis can yield evidence of shared vocabulary to trace influence between poets, we can build a network of different authors with their degree of influences. This can help a reader in finding a similar literature and in discovering implicit information.

In the period from 1813 to 1817, friends and fellow-poets Lord Byron and Thomas Moore wrote a series of long poems which are now seen as representative of Romantic Orientalism (a subset of Romantic literature recognisable by its Oriental and Middle-Eastern themes and settings). Throughout this period, an unusual pattern of coincidence is evident in the writings of the two poets, with correspondence between the poets describing similar plots, settings, and characters names in their respective works. The publication of Byron's quartet of Oriental tales in 1813 and 1814 (*The Giaour, The Bride of Abydos, The Corsair, Lara*) anticipated much of the substance of Moore's work, and delayed the publication of his own suite of four Oriental poems, *Lalla Rookh*, until 1817. On the publication of the latter, many reviewers accused Moore of imitating Byron's work, correctly fulfilling Moore's own prediction of 1813, that he would be seen as "an humble follower–a Byronian" (Moore, 1964). Subsequent critics have generally acknowledged Byron as a direct influence on Moore, but the basis of these acknowledgements is usually subjective critical interpretation of plot, character, and poetic form in the published texts (see, in particular, (Vail, 2001), (Sultana, 1989), (Gregory, 2008)). More general accounts of Byron's and Moore's literary association can be found in (Hamilton, 1948), (Jordan, 1948), (Tessier, 2014).

The purpose of this project is to investigate further the possible causes for the unusual pattern of coincidence in the writings of these two poets during this time. A Computational Linguistics approach to Byron's and Moore's Orientalism was identified as a potentially productive way of studying coincidence, influence, and imitation between their writings and how they related to the genre of Romantic Orientalism. Fresh empirical insight into this topic is desirable because of the difficulty of thinking about and articulating these issues in a way that is not speculative or nebulous. Such methodologies have not been applied to these texts, and offer the possibility of yielding fresh perspectives on questions about the texts, and the genre of Romantic Orientalism: is it defined by a limited vocabulary which inevitably leads to similarities and coincidences between its practitioners? Does writing within a specific genre impose topical or semantic constraint upon the author?

The motivations for the project emerge from a conviction that Computational Linguistics techniques may reveal evidence of shared vocabulary or formal textual characteristics in the works of Byron and Moore during the period 1813-17. The questions that the project seeks to answer include: can we identify and trace Byron's influence on Moore's writings? Did Moore imitate Byron, as many reviewers of the time suggested? Is there a shared vocabulary of Romantic Orientalism? Is it possible to characterise a literary genre in these terms, rather than in terms of plot, character, theme, etc.? The basis for such enquiries must go beyond a subjective comparison of the poems: the method that has characterised literary-critical approaches to these texts to date.

2 Distributional semantics

How related are love and emotion? Reasoning about semantic relatedness of natural language text is not a very difficult task for a human because of sufficient background knowledge and other related information to understand the semantics of natural language text. However, for computers, it is still an open issue to provide significant background knowledge to understand the complex structure of natural language. One plausible way to provide such background knowledge is taking the usage of given text in large contextual space into account.

Semantic relatedness of two given terms (text fragments, phrases or words) can be obtained by calculating the correlation between two high dimensional vectors of a Distributional Semantic Model (DSM), which is based on the assumption that semantic meaning of a text can be inferred from its usage in context (Harris, 1954), i.e. its distribution in text. DSM builds this semantic representation through a statistical analysis over the large contextual information in which a term occurs (see for details (Landauer, 1998), (Blei, 2003)). One recent popular model to calculate this semantic relatedness by using the distributional semantics is Explicit Semantic Analysis (ESA) proposed by (Gabrilovich and Markovitch, 2007), which attempts to represent the semantics of the given term by a high dimensional vector in explicit concept space such as Wikipedia concepts. Every explicit concept represents a dimension of the ESA vector, and associativity weight of a given term with the explicit concept reflects the vector dimension weight. For instance, for a given term t, ESA builds a vector v, where $v = \sum_{i=0}^{N} a_i * c_i$ and c_i is i^{th} concept from the explicit concept space, and a_i is the associativity weight of term t with the concept c_i. Here, N represents the total number of concepts. The semantic relatedness score is calculated by taking cosine between the corresponding high dimensional vectors.

3 Approach

Section 1 described our aim to investigate whether textual analysis techniques can yield evidence about Byron's influence on Moore's writings by analyzing the four long poems (published in 1813-14) by Lord Byron and a collection of four long poems (published in 1817) by Thomas Moore. To analyze this influence, we calculate semantic relatedness scores between Byron's poems and Moore's poems. We split these poems in line-groups[1] and obtain 227 line-groups from Byron's poems and 246 line-groups from Moore's poems. We calculate ESA scores of every line-group of Byron's poems with every line-group of Moore's poems. All the line-group pairs can be sorted according to their relatedness scores, which can provide highly related line-group pairs. After getting these highly related pairs, we can manually analyze them, and if manual analysis confirms the high relatedness of the pairs provided by ESA, then it may indicate some degree of influence or imitation between the poets. Also, these results will conclude that text analysis techniques can reduce the human effort in analyzing the influence between work by different authors.

4 Evaluation

4.1 Experiment

We built two ESA models; one by using Wikipedia and the other by using a corpus of poetry primarily from the eighteenth and nineteenth centuries[2]. In the first model, we take every Wikipedia article as a dimension of the ESA vector, and TF-IDF weight of a given text with article content is considered as the associativity strength with the corresponding dimension. We use modified ESA (Aggarwal, 2012) which builds the ESA vector by taking all words of a given text together rather than taking them individually. Wikipedia may not have a good coverage of the vocabulary of poems in Romantic Orientalism, which led us to try another ESA model that utilizes a Poetic Corpus. This corpus consists of 892 long poems and some of the poems contain more than 7K lines. Therefore, we split each poem with their line-groups and obtain 22K different line-groups. Similar to Wikipedia-based ESA, we take every line-group as a dimension of the ESA vector, and TF-IDF weight of the given text with line-group is considered as associativity strength with the corresponding dimension.

We use both ESA models: Wikipedia-based ESA and Poetic Corpus-based ESA to calculate the semantic relatedness scores of every line-group of Byron's poems with every line-group of Moore's poems. Both the results obtained by these two models are analyzed manually to check if Poetic Corpus-based ESA outperforms Wikipedia-based ESA as Poetic Corpus has better vocabulary coverage for Romantic Orientalism poems. We described in section 3 that we obtain 227 line-groups from Byron's poems and 246 line-groups from Moore's poems that means 56K line-group pairs. Manual analysis of 56K line-group pairs will take a very long time, therefore, we analyze only a small subset of the 56K pairs. To select the sample, we categorize the line-group pairs in three different categories: Highly-Related, May-be-Related and Not-Related. In the ranked list of line-group pairs, the top 1K are considered Highly-Related, the pairs ranked between 25K to 26K are considered May-be-Related, and the bottom 1K are taken as Not-Related. We randomly selected 5 line-group pairs from each category and manually analyzed the results obtained from ESA. Hence, we analyzed 15 pairs obtained according to Wikipedia-based ESA and 15 pairs according to PoeticCorpus-based ESA.

4.2 Results and Discussion

Manual (close-reading) analysis of 15 line-group pairs from the Wikipedia-based ESA took place first. At first glance, the pairs identified as Highly-Related were indeed quite closely related, particularly in terms of their narrative content. While some individual line-groups appeared in more than one pairing identified by the model, the pair exhibited a frequently occurring narrative scenario where a female character addressed her male lover before the departure or death of one of the parties. The model also succeeded in identifying this scenario in poems by both Byron and Moore. The scenes are unsurprisingly united by the presence of strong emotional language and imagery on the theme of love. However, the recognition of a leavetaking (whether in death or departure) in the scenes is also noteworthy, as is the fact that the identified line-groups are comprised of direct quotations from characters (as opposed to poetic narrative).

[1]Line-groups in poetry are similar to paragraphs in prose. On the printed page, a line of white space separates one line group from the next. Like paragraphs, they vary in length, and are often semantically, syntactically, or thematically self-contained.

[2]The poems in this corpus come from Women Writers Project (1560-1845), Eighteenth-Century Collections Online (1701-1800), and poetic corpora shared by Ted Underwood (1701-1899)

Subjected to manual analysis, pairs of line-groups in the May-be-Related and Not-Related categories exhibit varying degrees of relatedness. Most are lacking the immediate recognition of narrative similarity evident in the Highly-Related pairs, with some pairs containing vastly different narrative scenarios. Many of the consistencies from the Highly-Related category are also absent: some pairs vary greatly in length, and some contain a mix of narrative and quotation. One example from the manually-analysed examples proved to be a potential anomaly: a pair determined by the model to be Not-Related (i.e. in the bottom 1K of pairs in terms of relatedness) might easily be considered related in that both line-groups are florid poetic descriptions of a pastoral landscape.

The results of the Poetic Corpus-based ESA model were similar, if a little more refined. Interestingly, the line-group pairs in the Highly-Related category were largely similar to those resulting from the Wikipedia-based ESA. They were comprised of direct quotation (rather than narrative), and featured a character speaking to their lover in strong emotional language. In some cases (though not consistently) greater linguistic similarities between the pairings were more evident than in the results of the Wikipedia-based ESA. This was an anticipated consequence of using the Poetic Corpus-based ESA, where the model would be more likely to recognise the more unconventional features of nineteenth-century poetic diction than the Wikipedia-based ESA.

From a literary-critical perspective, however, identification of the Highly-Related pairs by a computer is no great advance on the capabilities of human scholarship. A traditional scholar can just as easily recognise the similarities in the scenes identified by both the Wikipedia- and Poetic Corpus-based ESAs in the course of reading the eight poems by Byron and Moore. Their narrative similarity is the most prominent characteristic that contributes to their relatedness. This identification can be made by the lone scholar because the dataset is relatively small in this project, and the time needed to read and analyse it is not prohibitive. The potential value of this kind of automated semantic-relatedness identification is increased when it is applied in a more exploratory fashion to larger datasets, and to poetic corpora whose scales are beyond the reasonable comprehension of the individual scholar. In this scenario, a potential application of the process would involve identifying and mapping the patterns and networks of relatedness in large-scale poetic corpora. For the present purposes of this project–studying imitation and influence in the texts of Byron and Moore–semantic relatedness measurements have been of limited value on their own, but have offered promise in other areas. The first aspect of their success has been in identifying sentiment analysis as a potential next step in drilling down into the texts to further reveal the essence of their similarity. The second is revealing a wider application of semantic relatedness in examining broader patterns of similarity within the history of poetry.

5 Conclusions and Future Work

We developed a method to identify influence and imitation in Romantic Orientalism poetry. We built two Explicit Semantic Analysis (ESA) models by using Wikipedia and a Poetic Corpus. The results from the analysis conducted with the Poetic Corpus-based ESA were a slight improvement on those resulting from the Wikipedia-based ESA. This was as anticipated, and results might be improved even further with a refined Poetic Corpus comprised of works from a more concentrated time period, which are more likely to share linguistic similarities with the Byron and Moore poems.

The performance of ESA model depends on several parameters (Aggarwal, 2014) that are included in the model, therefore, future work will include an investigation of ESA model in literature research. Also, we are planning to use an improved version of the ESA (Polajnar, 2013) model which reduce the orthogonality problem in the model. The value of ESA to the particular task of tracing imitation and influence in the Romantic Orientalist poetry of Byron and Moore has been limited thus far, but it has provided evidence of linguistic similarities in the expression of emotion. The next step for further investigation of imitation and influence between the two poets will involve the use of sentiment analysis. ESA was successful in identifying line groups that were closely related in terms of their narrative content and in their use of similarly emotional language. For such a small dataset, this does not represent a significant improvement on close reading, as similar results could have been obtained in this manner quite quickly. But the automated identification of semantic relatedness demonstrated in this project has potentially valuable applications for exploring broader literary corpora. For instance, a semantic mapping of transnational and transhistorical poetic relatedness is a possible future venue for our research.

Acknowledgments

This work has been funded in part by a research grant from Science Foundation Ireland (SFI) under Grant Number SFI/12/RC/2289 (INSIGHT) and by the EU FP7 program in the context of the project LIDER (610782).

References

Harris, Zellig, *Distributional structure*, 1954. Word 10 (23): 146-162.

Gabrilovich, Evgeniy and Markovitch, Shaul, *Computing semantic relatedness using Wikipedia-based explicit semantic analysis*, 2007. Proceedings of the 20th international joint conference on Artifical intelligence Hyderabad, India 1606–1611

Landauer, Thomas K and Foltz, Peter W and Laham, Darrell, An introduction to latent semantic analysis, Discourse processes, 25, 2-3, 259–284, 1998, Taylor & Francis

Blei, David M and Ng, Andrew Y and Jordan, Michael I Latent dirichlet allocation, the Journal of machine Learning research, 3, 993–1022, 2003, JMLR. org

Aggarwal, Nitish and Asooja, Kartik and Buitelaar, Paul DERI&UPM: Pushing corpus based relatedness to similarity: Shared task system description., Proceedings of the First Joint Conference on Lexical and Computational Semantics-Volume 1: Proceedings of the main conference and the shared task, and Volume 2: Proceedings of the Sixth International Workshop on Semantic Evaluation. Association for Computational Linguistics, 2012.

Ramsay, Stephen *Reading Machines: Toward an Algorithmic Criticism*, Urbana: University of Illinois Press, 2011. Print.

Moore, Thomas The Letters of Thomas Moore, Ed. Wilfred S. Dowden. 2 vols. Oxford: Clarendon Press, 1964. Print.

Gregory, Allan, "Thomas Moore's Orientalism." *Byron and Orientalism*, Ed. Peter Cochran. Newcastle upon Tyne: Cambridge Scholars, 2008. 173-82. Print.

Hamilton, Ian, "Byron and the Best of Friends." *Keepers of the Flame Literary Estates and the Rise of Biography.* London: Hutchinson, 1992. Print.

Jordan, Hoover H., "Byron and Moore." *Modern Language Quarterly*, 9.4 (1948): 429-39. Print.

Sultana, Fehmida, "Romantic Orientalism and Islam: Southey, Shelley, Moore, and Byron.", Unpublished dissertation. Tufts University, 1989. Print.

Polajnar, Tamara and Aggarwal, Nitish and Asooja, Kartik and Buitelaar, Paul, *Improving ESA with document similarity*, *Advances in Information Retrieval*, 582–593, 2013, Springer

Aggarwal, Nitish and Asooja, Kartik and Buitelaar, Paul *Exploring ESA to Improve Word Relatedness*, *Third Joint Conference on Lexical and Computational Semantics (*SEM)*, 2014

Tessier, Therese, "Byron and Thomas Moore: A Great Literary Friendship.", *The Byron Journal* 20 (1992): 4658. MetaPress. Web. 22 Jan. 2014.

Vail, Jeffery W., *The Literary Relationship of Lord Byron & Thomas Moore*, Baltimore: Johns Hopkins University Press, 2001. Print.

Unsupervised Approach to Extracting Problem Phrases from User Reviews of Products

Elena Tutubalina[1] and **Vladimir Ivanov**[1,2,3]
[1]Kazan (Volga region) Federal University, Kazan, Russia
[2]Institute of Informatics, Tatarstan Academy of Sciences, Kazan, Russia
[3]National University of Science and Technology "MISIS", Moscow, Russia
{tutubalinaev,nomemm}@gmail.com

Abstract

This paper describes an approach to problem phrase extraction from texts that contain user experience with products. In contrast to other works, we propose a straightforward approach to problem phrase extraction based on syntactic and semantic connections between a problem indicator and mentions about the problem targets. In this paper, we discuss (i) grammatical dependencies between the target and the problem indicators and (ii) a number of domain-specific targets that were extracted using problem phrase structure and additional world knowledge. The algorithm achieves an average F1-measure of 77%, evaluated on reviews about electronic and automobile products.

1 Introduction

Automatic analysis of reviews can increase information about product effectiveness. This is especially important to a company if the information can be obtained with minimal costs. Customers write reviews regarding product issues that are too difficult to handle without technical support.

In this paper, we present a study about connections between a product (the target of a problem phrase) and words (problem indicators), describing unexpected situations specific to products. We define problem indicators as words describing phrases that contain obvious links to a problem (e.g., *problem, issue*). We also define problem indicators as words that mention implicit problems (e.g., *after, sometimes*). The problem indicator may be presented as an action verb with a negation expressing product failure.

The task is to identify which noun phrases (NPs) referred to the problem target in the sentence. The task is divided into two subtasks: (1) identify what phrase potentially contains information about a problem and (2) find possible targets using the set of nouns for a given problem expression. The first subtask, problem phrase identification, determines whether a given sentence contains problem phrases. The second subtask, target phrase extraction, identifies the targets of a given problem phrase.

The problem indicators are significant for problem sentences where the device doesn't work correctly. However, the presence of indicators in the sentence may have insufficient context to determine the problem's existence. In examples 1 and 2, the object that receives the action isn't defined ("I have not seen one", "something hasn't been right").

1. After looking for months, I have not seen one that I like at the local store and have expanded to other local stores.
2. Something hasn't been right for sometimes now - we have advised the support staff several times about this issue.

We present the dependency-based approach for extracting problem phrases and its target from user reviews of products. We suppose that problem indicators have a syntax connection with the target of a problem phrase. Domain-specific targets are extracted by determining a domain category of related target words in WordNet.

The rest of the paper is organized as follows. In section 2, we introduce related work in different areas of text classification of reviews and target detection. Section 3 describes our approach and classifies dependency relations between problem indicators and targets of problem phrases. We present experimental results in section 4. Section 5 presents our conclusions and future extensions of this work.

2 Related Work

Several different methods have been proposed in literature for the classification of product reviews in different areas of research. The primary area of related works is sentiment analysis. Turney (2002) presented an unsupervised learning algorithm for classifying reviews from a consumer platform on the Web. The author extracted phrases containing adjectives or adverbs from reviews of different domains. His algorithm achieved 74% accuracy for 410 reviews sampled from four different domains. Popescu and Etzioni (2007) focused on entity-level classification using extraction rules on sentences with features or entities. They proposed a method for opinion phrase extraction based on the semantic orientation of words in the context of product features. Authors commonly focused on explicit product features from noun phrases. They reported a recall of 89% and a precision of 86% for opinion phrase polarity determination with known product features and a precision of 79% and a recall of 76% for product feature identification. Hu et al. (2004) extracted sentences that contained one or more product features and identified the polarity of the opinion sentences using the adjective set from WordNet.

Another group of related works explores extracting information about subjectivity. Wiebe and Wilson (2002) recognized opinionated and evaluative (subjective) language in text. According to them, a sentence is subjective if it contains a significant expression of emotion, opinion, or an idea about why something has happened. Wilson et al. (2004) used dependency relations classifying the subjectivity of deeply nested clauses for their task of classifying the strength of the opinions. Breck (2007) used semi-supervised sequence modeling by conditional random fields (CRF) for entity-level opinion expressions. The best F1-measure (70.65%) was achieved for identifying opinion expressions.

There is much research on finding targets of objects using dependency relations (Quadir (2009); Lu (2010); Qiu et al. (2011)). Qadir (2009) identified opinion sentences that were specific to product features. The words forming the dependency relations were analyzed for frequent product feature. Qadir tagged each sentence with only one product feature. In contrast, we propose that problem phrases have multiple targets. Qiu et al. (2011) extracted sentiment words and aspects by using syntactic relations. They described a propagation approach that achieved a recall of 83% and a precision of 88%.

Problem detection and extraction of problem phrases from texts are less studied. We used a clause-based approach to problem-phrase extraction from user reviews of products. This method is based on dictionaries and rules and performed well compared to the simple baseline given by supervised machine learning algorithms. They achieved a recall of 77% and a precision of 74% for user reviews about electronic products. The current task of this research is identifying the targets of problem phrases to reduce classification errors. Gupta (2013) studied the extraction of problems with AT&T products and services from English Twitter messages. The author used a supervised method to train a maximum entropy classifier. Gupta reported the best performance F1-measure of 75% for identification of problem target. In contrast, our method is based on grammatical domain-independent relations in a sentence.

3 Target Extraction

In this section, we describe our method for extracting problem phrases, related to targets, from customer reviews. PW is an initially empty set of the problem indicators, T is an empty target set. The common approach starts from an initially empty set of pairs (problem indicator, target), $PTWs = (PW, T)$, where $PW = T = \emptyset$. The approach is divided into three steps: problem-phrase identification, target extraction, and domain-specific target detection. After three steps, the algorithm marks the sentence as a problem sentence if at least one pair (indicator, target) is extracted (i.e. $PTWs = \{(pw_1, t_1), (pw_2, t_2), ...\}$, $pw_i \in PW, t_i \in T$). We describe problem-phrase identification in section 3.1. Section 3.2 describes dependency relations for target extraction. Section 3.3 explains identifying domain-specific targets using semantic knowledge from WordNet.

3.1 Problem Phrase Identification

A common appoach to problem-phrase extraction uses problem indicators (i.e., words, that indicate a problem in a sentence). We briefly describe the manually created ProblemWord dictionary, defined in Ivanov and Tutubalina (2014). The ProblemWord dictionary includes problem indicators such as *problem*, *error*, *failure*, *malfunction*, *crash*, *break*, *reboot*, *have to replace*, etc. We collected synonyms for these problem indicators. The manually created dictionary consists of about 300 terms.

Problem-phrase identification. In this step, the algorithm looks for the problem indicators in the sentence. The algorithm looks for verb phrases headed by an action verb with a negation or looks for problem words from manually created dictionaries (without related negations). As a result, the set PW is collected, which includes all problem indicators $pw_i \in PW$, found in the sentence S.

3.2 Dependency Relations for Target Extraction

The method for target extraction uses syntax dependencies to determine connections between possible targets and problem indicators. The phrase describing the problem is a combination of the target and the problem indicators. The structure of a sentence with selected collapsed dependencies is shown in Figure 1. We use the Stanford typed dependencies from the Stanford parser[1]. For this sentence, the Stanford dependencies representation with the selected problem indicator is {*dobj(use, firefox), nn(software, printer), prep_with(use, software), vmod(software, added), pre_to(added, computer)*}. These dependencies are written as relation_type(head, dependent), where the head and the dependent have a dependency direction associated with them in the sentence.

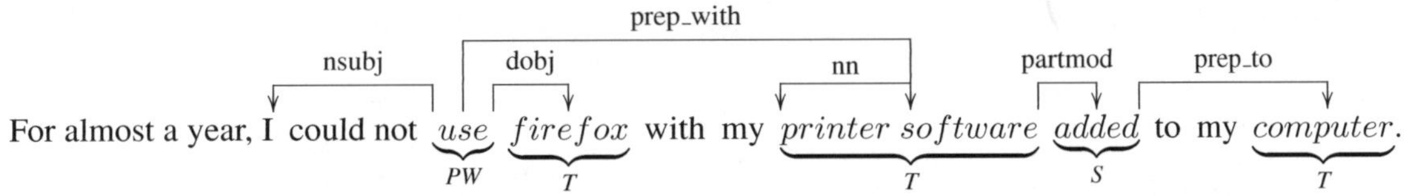

Figure 1: The syntactic structure of a sentence with collapsed dependencies.

To identify connections between the problem indicator and the targets of problem phrase, we use direct and indirect dependency relations between two words that are defined in (Qiu et. al., 2011). The intuition behind a choice of these types is that only syntactically and semantically rich mentions of targets are extracted, reducing noise in the extracted set of nouns. The direct dependencies allow for recognizing some relations directly between the target and the problem indicator. Indirect dependency indicates that one word depends on the other word through some additional words, which we call *successors*. A successor word connects to a problem indicator and replaces a problem indicator in relation with a target. The connection of the successor with the problem indicator and the target can possibly indicate the relation between the indicator and the target of the problem phrase through context.

Sentences 3–4 show examples with direct and indirect dependency relations taken from the review sentences. PW refers to a problem indicator, and T refers to a target of a problem phrase, S refers to a successor of a problem indicator. In example 3, *give* is the action verb with the related negation, which indicates the problem and has a direct connection with the target *stars*. Example 4 contains problems with the *cord*, and there is no problems with domain-specific products in example 3.

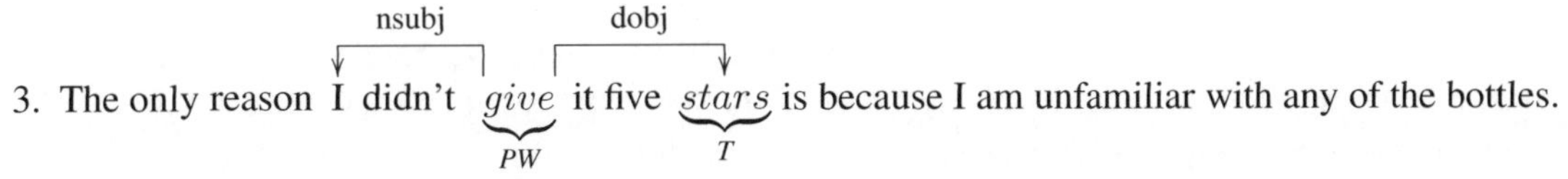

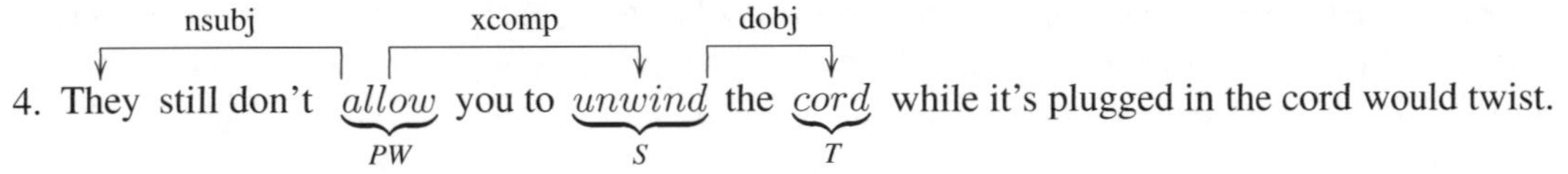

[1]http://nlp.stanford.edu/software/lex-parser.shtml

Target extraction. In second step, for each problem indicator $pw_i \in PW$ the approach extracts all related targets. The targets are found in the dependencies representation of the sentence S. The target is related to the problem word if there is direct or indirect dependency between the target word and the problem indicator or the problem indicator's successor, respectively, in the sentence representation. We add to the set $PWTs$ one $pair(pw_i, t_j)$ for each target t_j, i.e., $PWTs = PWTs \cup \{pair(pw_i, t_j)\}$, $T = T \cup \{t_j\}$.

3.3 Domain-Specific Target Detection Using WordNet Categories

Domain-specific targets can be extracted by using additional world knowledge. Domain-specific targets are objects that have important meanings in a particular domain. The method uses WordNet for choosing domain-specific targets. WordNet organizes related words in synsets as synonym sets. It extracts domain categories from WordNet for selected problem targets in the sentence. WordNet assigns multiple domain semantic labels to terms in the domain. The method extracts categories for each target and its hypernyms, hyponyms, and holonyms. A hyponym is a lexical relation between a more general term and a more particular term (e.g., *machine/computer*). A hypernym is a word that is more generic than a given entity (e.g., *portable computer/laptop*). A holonym is a term that denotes a complete object whose part is denoted by given word (e.g., *computer/keyboard*).

Figure 2 shows the relations that classified targets into WordNet domains. Each target from the problem phrase is represented by a row in the first table. Hyponym, hypernym and holonym relations are drawn between rows in the tables. Dashed arrows are represented type-of relations, and solid arrows are represented part-of relations between the target and the WordNet synset. Solid lines are represented links to the WordNet domain category. In the example, the target *TouchPad* has an unknown category.

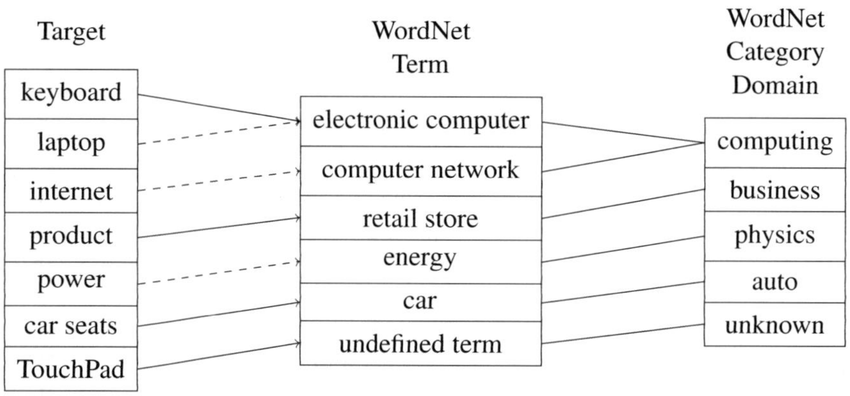

Figure 2: The example of relating targets into WordNet categories

Domain-specific target detection. In the third step, the algorithm reduces pairs with non-domain-specific problem targets from the set $PWTs$ using semantic knowledge. The pair $pair(pw_i, t_j)$ is reduced if there is no term with a domain category in the hierarchy of WordNet synsets induced by the hypernym, hyponym, or holonym relations with target t_j.

4 Evaluation and Discussion

For our experiments we collected 734 sentences from the HP website[2]. We employed 953 sentences from Amazon reviews[3] about automobile products. Of the total sentences, 1,288 sentences (506 + 782 from electronic and automobile domains) were classified as problem sentences, and 399 (228 + 171) sentences were labeled as part of the no-problem class. Class labels for each sentence were obtained by using the Amazon Mechanical Turk service. Each sentence does not have any particular label for targets and contains at least one problem indicator that the approach can find. We propose that the problem

[2]http://reviews.shop.hp.com

[3]The dataset is available at https://snap.stanford.edu/data/web-Amazon.html

phrase with the problem indicator always has targets, but not necessarily domain-specific targets. For our performance metrics, we view that a text classification task is to identify whether a target is a domain-specific problem target. We computed precision (P), recall (R), accuracy (Acc.) and F1-mesure (F1).

Type of targets	Examples
Domain-specific	internet, printer, monitor, screen, laptop, processor, driver
Undefined category	Apple, HP printer, win7, printhead, adapter, reboots
Other targets	marketing, stars, box, unit, letters, shipment, results

Table 1: Problem targets related to WordNet categories.

Table 1 gives examples of the problem targets that are extracted in connection with problem indicators and are related to the categories. The total number of targets extracted from 506 problem sentences about electronic products were 258 domain-specific targets, 458 targets without a WordNet category and 138 other targets. The approach collected 151 compound targets (e.g., *auto configuration*, *network settings*), that were related to the undefined category.

We used different methods to compare the performance of our approach, as follows:

1. We considered the targets extracted by direct dependencies (we did not use any lexical knowledge).
2. We considered all targets extracted by direct and indirect dependencies as domain-specific targets.
3. We considered only domain-specific targets extracted by direct and indirect dependencies. We extracted the targets, if the selected target was a term related to computing, electronic, or automobile terminology from WordNet. We also considered the targets that don't relate to any WordNet category and did not have a lexical meaning such as "time" or "person".

Method name	Electronics				Cars			
	P	R	Acc.	F1	P	R	Acc.	F1
Direct Dependencies	.74	.48	.53	.58	.83	.67	.62	.74
+ Indirect Dependencies	.73	.90	.71	.81	.83	.92	.78	.87
+ WordNet caterogies	.74	.71	.62	.72	.84	.79	.70	.81

Table 2: Performance metrics of the dependency-based approach.

Performance metrics are calculated with this dataset and provided in able 2. The average recall and the average precision of problem-phrase extraction related to domain-specific targets are 75% and 79%, respectively. WordNet is limited and does not include many proper nouns (e.g., *MacBook*, *Honda Odyssey*) related to a particular domain. Thus, domain-specific target detection using WordNet categories led to a decrease in the average recall (from 91% to 75%). Another type of sentence, that decreases the average recall, is user sentences with a situation description, not just a report about a problem ("Something hasn't been right for sometimes now", for example).

5 Conclusion

In this paper, we aim to identify problem phrases and to connect the proper targets of phrases with problems or difficult situations. Without using domain-specific knowledge about products, we focus our attention on dependency-based syntactic information between the target and the problem indicators in the text. We use WordNet synsets with domain labels to reduce targets that aren't related to a product domain. The average value of the F1-measure (about 84% for all targets and 77% for domain-specific targets) is better than the F1-measure in Ivanov and Tutubalina (2014). Our research shows that dependencies and syntactic information combine with each other to collect different parts of problem targets for target phrase extraction. For future work, we plan to extend the evaluation corpus with new domains to explore more kinds of syntactic information between problem indicators and the dependent context.

References

Turney P. D. 2002. *Thumbs up or thumbs down?: semantic orientation applied to unsupervised classification of reviews.* Association for Computational Linguistics, 417–424.

Popescu A. M., Etzioni O. 2007. *Extracting product features and opinions from reviews.* //Natural language processing and text mining, Springer, London, 9–28.

Hu M., Liu B. 2004. *Mining and summarizing customer reviews.* Proceedings of the tenth ACM SIGKDD international conference on Knowledge discovery and data mining, 168–177.

Wiebe J., Wilson T. 2002. *Learning to disambiguate potentially subjective expressions.* Proceedings of the 6th conference on Natural language learning-Volume 20, Association for Computational Linguistics, 1–7.

Wilson T., Wiebe J., Hwa R. 2004. *Just how mad are you? Finding strong and weak opinion clauses.* Aaai, 761–769.

Breck E., Choi Y., Cardie C. 2007. *Identifying Expressions of Opinion in Context.* IJCAI, 2683–2688.

Narenda Gupta. 2013. *Extracting phrases describing problems with products and services from twitter messages.* Conference on Intelligent Text Processing and Computational Linguistics, CICling2013.

Ivanov V., Tutubalina E. 2014. *Clause-based approach to extracting problem phrases from user reviews of products.* Proceeding of the 3d International Conference on Analysis of Images, Social Networks, and Texts AIST'14, Russia, 2014.

Lu B. 2010. *Identifying opinion holders and targets with dependency parser in Chinese news texts.* Proceedings of the NAACL HLT 2010 Student Research Workshop. Association for Computational Linguistics, 46–51.

Qadir A. 2009. *Detecting opinion sentences specific to product features in customer reviews using typed dependency relations.* Proceedings of the Workshop on Events in Emerging Text Types. Association for Computational Linguistics, 38–43.

G. Qiu, B. Liu, J. Bu, C. Chen 2011. *Opinion word expansion and target extraction through double propagation.* Computational linguistics, 9–27.

Extracting a Repository of Events and Event References from News Clusters

Silvia Julinda
TU Berlin
Einsteinufer 17
Berlin, Germany
silvia.julinda@gmail.com

Christoph Boden
TU Berlin
Einsteinufer 17
Berlin, Germany
christoph.boden@tu-berlin.de

Alan Akbik
TU Berlin
Einsteinufer 17
Berlin, Germany
alan.akbik@tu-berlin.de

Abstract

In this paper, we prose to build a repository of events and event references from clusters of news articles. We present an automated approach that is based on the hypothesis that if two sentences are *a)* found in the same cluster of news articles and *b)* contain temporal expressions that reference the same point in time, they are likely to refer to the same event. This allows us to group similar sentences together and apply open-domain Information Extraction (OpenIE) methods to extract lists of textual references for each detected event. We outline our proposed approach and present a preliminary evaluation in which we extract events and references from 20 clusters of online news. Our experiments indicate that for the largest part our hypothesis holds true, pointing to a strong potential for applying our approach to building an event repository. We illustrate cases in which our hypothesis fails and discuss ways for addressing sources or errors.

1 Introduction

We present ongoing work in the automatic creation of a repository of events and event references from clusters of online news articles. In the context of this work, an *event* is something that happens at one specific point in time that can be referenced in text with different text surface forms. An example of this may be the acquisition of WhatsApp by Facebook, which has a specific timestamp (02-19-2014), as well as a number of different textual references (such as "the acquisition of WhatsApp", "Facebook's landmark deal" etc). Unlike previous work in event extraction (Aone and Ramos-Santacruz, 2000; Ji and Grishman, 2008), we are less interested in filling slots in a fixed set of event templates. Rather, we aim to identify an unrestricted set of events (Ritter et al., 2012) and all their possible event mentions. This means that even noun phrases ("the much-discussed takeover") and incomplete mentions ("Zuckerberg's 19 billion bet") are valid textual references we wish to capture.

We give examples of such events in Table 1. We believe that automatically distilling such events from news text and hosting them in an event repository could provide a valuable resource to gain a comprehensive overview of world events and also serve as a resource for *event-linking* efforts in future Information Extraction (IE) research.

In this paper, we propose a method for automatically creating such an event repository. Our method leverages computer-generated news sites that aggregate articles from news sources worldwide and group similar stories into news clusters. Such news clusters represent an intriguing reservoir for event extraction: Each cluster typically represents one *news item* that is reported on by hundreds of different online sources. Articles in a cluster will therefore describe similar information content - and reference the same events - using different words. On these news articles, we apply temporal expression taggers to identify and normalize textual references to specific points in time.

Our main hypothesis is that if two sentences are *a)* found in the same cluster of news articles and *b)* contain temporal expressions that reference the same point in time, they are likely to refer to the same event. This allows us to group similar sentences together and for each referenced point in time extract an event with a list of different textual references.

ID	TIMESTAMP	REPRESENTATIVE	TEXTUAL REFERENCES
1	2014-02-19	Facebook buys WhatsApp	Facebook buying WhatsApp the landmark deal Zuckerberg's acquisition of the mobile messaging-service
2	2014-02-01	Rosetta transmits message	Rosetta sends signal to Earth the spacecraft's first message the message from the Rosetta spacecraft
3	2014-02-07	Sinabung volcano erupts	Indonesian volcano unleashed a major eruption the eruption of Mount Sinabung volcano its biggest eruption yet

Table 1: Examples for events in the event repository. Each extracted event consists of an ID, a timestamp which indicates on which date the event took place, a short human-readable event representation, and a list of strings that may be used to reference this event.

In this paper, we present our event extraction system and conduct a preliminary evaluation in order to determine in how far our hypothesis holds. We discuss the evaluation results and possible improvements and give an outline of current and future work.

2 Event and Reference Extraction

2.1 Method Overview

Determine sentences likely to reference the same event. We begin the event extraction process by crawling Google News[1] to retrieve clusters of English language news articles and their publishing date. Each news article is then boilerplated and segmented into sentences.
We then make use of temporal expression taggers (Strötgen and Gertz, 2010; Chang and Manning, 2012) to recognize temporal expressions in text and normalize them into machine-readable timestamps. This causes expressions such as "last Friday", "winter of 2013", and "Saturday morning" to be normalized to the timestamps "2013-10-10", "2013-WI", and "2012-09-24TMO" respectively by using the article's publishing date as a reference point. We identify all sentences with temporal expressions and group sentences together that *a)* contain the same timestamp and *b)* are found in the same cluster of documents. Refer to Table 2 for examples of sentences grouped according to these criteria.
Determine Open-Domain Facts. Because sentences may refer to multiple events[2], we use OpenIE methods (Schmitz et al., 2012; Choi, 2012) to determine for each sentence a list of N-ary facts. Each fact consist of a predicate and a number of arguments. We then discard all facts that do not contain the temporal expression in order to keep only those facts expressed within each sentence to which the temporal expression refers. This gives us a list of N-ary facts which we presume to refer to the same event, together with its timestamp.
Determine Event Representative and Store. For human readability purposes, we then identify a representative of the grouped N-ary facts by determining the most common predicate and head arguments. We assign a global ID to each event and store it along with its timestamp, its representative and a list of all textual references and their frequency counts in a database.

2.2 Granularity of Timestamps

One question at the onset of this work was which granularity of temporal expressions would be required. We manually inspected a sample of news clusters and noted that news articles rarely provide time information that is accurate to the minute. Rather, most temporal expressions refer to specific dates in past, present or future. We therefore choose the unit "day" as granularity for the temporal expressions in this work. We dismiss all expressions that refer to larger and more vague periods of time ("last winter",

[1] http://news.google.com/

[2] An example of this is the sentence: "*When asked, he said that WhatApp accepted Facebook's offer last Sunday*". Here, the temporal expression "*last Sunday*" refers only the "*WhatApp accepted Facebook's offer*" part of the sentence, not the date the person was asked.

TIMESTAMP	SENTENCES
2014-02-20	Facebook inked a deal **late Wednesday** to buy popular texting service WhatsApp.
	Yesterday , Facebook Chief Executive Officer Mark Zuckerberg bought their five-year-old company.
	Thursday , 20 February 2014 Facebook Inc will buy fast-growing mobile-messaging startup WhatsApp.
	Facebook Inc. agreed to buy mobile messaging-service WhatsApp **today** for as much as 19 billion.
2014-02-01	The European Space Agency received the all-clear message from its Rosetta spacecraft **at 7:18 p.m.**
	[..] a comet-chasing spacecraft sent its first signal back to Earth **on Monday**
	ESA received the all-clear message Hello World from its Rosetta spacecraft [..] away **shortly after 7 pm**.
	Yesterday's message from the Rosetta spacecraft was celebrated by scientists [..]
2014-02-07	Indonesia's Mount Sinabung volcano erupted and killed at least 11 people [..] **on Saturday**
	But **a day later** , Sinabung spewed hot rocks and ash up to 2km in the air.
	A giant cloud of hot volcanic ash clouds engulfs villages [..] in Sumatra island **on February 1, 2014**.
	An Indonesian volcano that has been rumbling for months unleashed a major eruption **Saturday**.

Table 2: Examples of sentences grouped by cluster and timestamp. The temporal expression taggers enable us to group sentences that refer to the same point of time in very different ways (highlighted bold). As can be seen in the examples, sentences grouped according to these criteria generally refer to the same event, albeit in sometimes widely varying words.

"throughout the year") and generalize all temporal information that refer to the time of day ("later today", "at 7:18 p.m.").

2.3 Improving Event Quality

Upon manual inspection of identified events we find that our hypothesis fails in some cases: A news item may often summarize a number of smaller events that happened within the same day. An example of this are news items that deal with unrest in war-torn countries that may reference several bombings, terrorist attacks and other violence that happened across the country on the day the article was published. Another example are sports articles that refer to several sport matches that take place during the same day. This is problematic, as in such cases we erroneously link non-synonymous textual references to the same event. We experiment with two methods for reducing this error:

Time Window Filter As indicated above, we note that our hypothesis most often fails for events that occur within 2 days of the publishing date of the articles in the news cluster. Accordingly, we experiment with filtering out such events, leaving only events to be extracted that lie in the more distant past or future (such as past or upcoming election days, significant events that impact the current news story). However, since the largest part of events that are reported on in online news take place within this 2-day time window, we risk significant recall-loss by discarding too many events.

Word Alignment Condition For this reason, we investigate requirements for facts to be grouped together in addition to the requirement of sharing the same timestamp. We experiment with monolingual word-alignment tools (Yao et al., 2013) to determine the "similarity" of two facts as the number of aligned content words. We then require at least one content word to be shared by two facts in order for them to be grouped together into an event.

3 Preliminary Evaluation

We conduct a preliminary evaluation to determine to which extend our hypothesis holds. To this end, we use our method to extract events from a sample of 20 news clusters with an average size of 200 news articles. We evaluate our method in four setups: *1)* The baseline setup in which we apply only the "*same cluster + same timestamp = same event*" hypothesis ("**BASE**"). *2)* The baseline setup plus the time window filter ("**TIME**"). *3)* The baseline setup plus the word alignment condition ("**ALIGN**"). *4)* The baseline setup plus both the time window filter and the word alignment condition ("**ALL**").

We manually evaluate each event found with our method by checking whether all references indeed refer to the same event. We calculate a *purity* value that indicates the proportion of the biggest group

METHOD	TOTAL EVENT REFERENCES	CORRECT EVENT REFERENCES	PRECISION	PURITY
BASE	**609**	511	0.839	0.698
TIME	109	88	0.807	0.699
ALIGN	**609**	**526**	**0.864**	**0.793**
ALL	109	89	0.817	0.728

Table 3: The results of our manual evaluation of extracted events and their event references. The main hypothesis that events mentioned with the same date in one cluster delivers quite promising results with 84% precision. The time window filter does not seem to contribute significant gains, while the ALIGN filter does boost both precision and purity.

of references that refer to the same event over all references in an event cluster. This means that if all references indeed refer to the same event, its purity is *1.0*. Table 3 lists the average purity over all events.

When a reference accurately represents both the content and the date contained in the original news sentence and the real world event mentioned actually occurred on this date, we labeled it as a "correct" event reference. The *precision* listed in Table 3 reflects the proportion of correct events references vs. all extracted event reference in the evaluation data set. This measure indicates how well the extraction itself performs, apart from the clustering of event references.

Hypothesis produces promising results with a precision of 0.84. In general, we find our underlying assumption to indeed be a good basis for event extraction. Our baseline approach based on only this hypothesis produces promising results with a precision of 0.84, albeit at somewhat low overall purity.

Wrong resolution of relative time references biggest source of error. When inspecting sources of errors more closely, we note that the approach fails most often because of erroneous resolution of relative time references such as *"yesterday", "past Saturday"* or *"this Sunday"*. This may happen because the wrong publishing date is assigned to a crawled news article, causing temporal taggers to use a wrong reference point for relative time expressions. With relative references to weekdays, the taggers are often unsure whether the past or present week is referenced. Consider the expression "*on Saturday*" in the sentence "*John Kerry will meet with opposition leaders on Saturday*". Although the coming Saturday is meant in this context, the temporal expression tagger normalizes the date to the last Saturday before the publishing date. We believe that such systematic errors can be addressed in future work through assigning higher confidence to explicit temporal expressions mentions and resolving ambiguities in relative expressions using this information.

Time Window Filter provides no significant contribution. Contrary to initial assumption filtering out events within a 2-day time window does not actually boost precision, but rather greatly reduces the total number of extracted events at slightly lower precision and purity. The likely reason for this behavior is the above noted most common error source is not addressed by this filter.

Word Alignment Condition boosts both precision and purity significantly. The word alignment condition on the other hand greatly increases both precision and purity. While the increase in purity is to be expected as different events occurring on the same date are indeed split into separate clusters, the increase in precision comes as somewhat of a surprise. Closer inspection of the results revealed that the word alignment approach aggressively groups similar event mentions, considering also synonyms as matches, therefore not resulting in redundant event detections as initially feared. Based on these results, we believe that experimentation with word alignment conditions may further increase event detection quality.

4 Conclusion

In this paper, we have proposed to create a repository of events and their textural references and presented an approach to accomplish this automatically by leveraging news clusters and temporal expressions. Our approach is based on the hypothesis that sentences that are found in the same news cluster and refer to the same point in time also refer to the same events. We described the implementation of a prototype system and conducted a preliminary manual evaluation on 20 news clusters to investigate our hypothesis.

Our findings generally point to a strong potential of automatically mining events and references from news clusters. While our hypothesis fails in some cases, our analysis indicates that incorporating monolingual word-alignment techniques can greatly improve extraction quality and appears to be a powerful tool to disambiguate events that share both timestamp and news cluster.

Present work focuses on further exploring the potential of word alignment as well as the use of cluster-wide statistics to correct labeling mistakes such as the ones observed for temporal tagging. We aim to use the system on very large amounts of news clusters crawled from the Web to generate - and make publicly available - the resource that we have proposed in this paper.

Acknowledgments

The research is funded by the European Union (EU) under grant no. 270137 'SCAPE' in the 7th Framework Program and the German Federal Ministry of Education and Research (BMBF) under grant no. 01ISI2033 'RADAR'.

References

Chinatsu Aone and Mila Ramos-Santacruz. 2000. Rees: a large-scale relation and event extraction system. In *Proceedings of the sixth conference on Applied natural language processing*, pages 76–83. Association for Computational Linguistics.

Angel X Chang and Christopher Manning. 2012. Sutime: A library for recognizing and normalizing time expressions. In *LREC*, pages 3735–3740.

J. D. Choi. 2012. Optimization of natural language processing components for robustness and scalability.

Heng Ji and Ralph Grishman. 2008. Refining event extraction through cross-document inference. In *ACL*, pages 254–262.

Alan Ritter, Oren Etzioni, Sam Clark, et al. 2012. Open domain event extraction from twitter. In *Proceedings of the 18th ACM SIGKDD international conference on Knowledge discovery and data mining*, pages 1104–1112. ACM.

Michael Schmitz, Robert Bart, Stephen Soderland, Oren Etzioni, et al. 2012. Open language learning for information extraction. In *Proceedings of the 2012 Joint Conference on Empirical Methods in Natural Language Processing and Computational Natural Language Learning*, pages 523–534. Association for Computational Linguistics.

Jannik Strötgen and Michael Gertz. 2010. Heideltime: High quality rule-based extraction and normalization of temporal expressions. In *Proceedings of the 5th International Workshop on Semantic Evaluation*, pages 321–324. Association for Computational Linguistics.

Xuchen Yao, Benjamin Van Durme, Chris Callison-Burch, and Peter Clark. 2013. A lightweight and high performance monolingual word aligner. In *Proceedings of ACL*.

Towards Social Event Detection and Contextualisation for Journalists

Prashant Khare
Insight Centre for Data Analytics
National University of Ireland,
Galway, Ireland

prashant.khare@insight-centre.org

Bahareh Rahmanzadeh Heravi
Insight Centre for Data Analytics
National University of Ireland,
Galway, Ireland

bahareh.heravi@insight-centre.org

Abstract

Social media platforms have become an important source of information in course of a breaking news event, such as natural calamity, political uproar, etc. News organisations and journalists are increasingly realising the value of information being propagated via social media. However, the sheer volume of the data produced on social media is overwhelming and manual inspection of this streaming data for finding, aggregation, and contextualising emerging event in a short time span is a day-to-day challenge by journalists and media organisations. It highlights the need for better tools and methods to help them utilise this user generated information for news production. This paper addresses the above problem for journalists by proposing an event detection and contextualisation framework that receives an input stream of social media data and generates the likely events in the form of clusters along with a certain context.

1 Introduction

Social media platforms have evolved to being more than just a user-to-user interaction channel, and play a prominent role in real-time information sharing. In many cases the real life 'events' are now shared and broadcast on the social media platforms, by normal citizens, and not professional journalists. This has turned the former consumer [only] of the news into [also] a broadcaster of the news, and thus the social media platforms into an invaluable source of newsworthy information. The news organisations are now more and more interested in gathering real-time information (such as breaking news, images, videos) by means of monitoring and harvesting the user-generated content (UGC). Survey results reveal that journalists are increasingly using social media platforms for their professional activities. For example surveys reveal that 96% of journalists in the UK and use feeds from social media in their work on a daily basis (Cision, 2013), 99% of Irish journalists use social media as a source of information in their work (Heravi et al., 2014), and 51% of journalists globally leverage microblogs to consume feeds for news and stories (Oriella, 2013). With the increasing usage of social media in the journalistic processes, it is critical for journalists to be able to filter the social streams to discover breaking news, and then analyse, aggregate, contextualise, and verify them in timely manner.

The concept of Social Semantic Journalism, introduced by Heravi et al. (2012), targets the above problems encountered by the media organisations. The Social Semantic Journalism framework (Heravi and McGinnis, 2013) utilises the social and semantic web technologies, and provides an integrated view for enhancing newsworthy information discovery, filtering, aggregation, verification and publication. While there is considerable work done to retrieve information from various sources of data (such as text) by various means, there is a paucity of tools available for detecting events from social media data and extracting relevant information about such events in the real time. Building upon the ideas of Social Semantic Journalism, to aid journalists in utilising UGC in an efficient manner, this paper proposes a framework that implements an event detection pipeline, which *clusters the data into different events,* and *determines the context of the events based on entities* (mentions particular to any person, place, event, or thing) related to the events. The information that flows on the social media is often via textual medium, and therefore in this proposed framework, we leverage text mining and Natural Language Processing (NLP) technologies to extract the information.

The remainder of this paper is organised as follows. Section 2 provides a background to the problem and briefly reviews related work. Section 3 presents our proposed Event Detection and Contextualisation framework and gives a detailed overview of its components and phases. Section 4 concludes the paper and discusses directions for future research.

2 Background and Related Work

Identifying new events, in the form of news from the data, is an area of interest for researchers for a long time. Topic detection and tracking (TDT) (Allan, 2002) focuses on breaking down a streaming text from newswire into smaller cohesive news pieces and determining if something has not been earlier reported. An event detection cycle is seen as a subtask within TDT (Allan, 2002). The data from social media platforms, such as Twitter, is quite voluminous and the streaming nature of this data warrants the usage of streaming algorithm models, where the data arrives in a chronological order (Muthukrishnan, 2005). The social media data is further processed in a bounded space and time, i.e. as every entry arrives it gets processed. Traditional approaches for identifying new information (an event) were to compare each new entry in the data with the previously arrived entries. Petrovic et al. (2010) investigated ways to identify tweets that first report the occurrence of an event by clustering mechanism to identify nearest neighbours in the textual data. This work has motivated many other contemporary research works to head in a related direction

Osborne et al. (2012) used the approach by Petrovic et al. (2010) as a baseline and investigated the ways to improve the event detection mechanism on Twitter data, by matching the frequency of newly occurring events from tweets with the activity (number of visits on a page) of the corresponding pages of entities from Wikipedia and analysed if there was a similar pattern observed while determining an event. Parikh and Karlapalem (2013), also considering frequency based analysis, developed an event detection system that extracts events from tweets by examining frequencies in the temporal blocks of streaming data.

Natural Language Processing (NLP) techniques can be leveraged in detecting events from voluminous social media data. Events are associated with entities and NLP techniques can be applied to extract the entities that are mentioned in the text that defines an event. To perform Named Entity Recognition (NER) on tweets Ritter et. al. (2011) redeveloped the taggers and segmenters of Stanford NLP library1. Ritter et al. (2012) extending the above work created an application Twical, that extracted an open domain calendar for events that were shared on Twitter.

For an event detection system, it is also crucial to determine the context of a piece of text/information. The contextualisation is answering the question ‘what is this about?’ and one of the ways to answer it could be by aggregating information from knowledge base such as Wikipedia (SanJuan et al., 2012). A potential context of the content can likely be inferred by extracting set of topics that bound the text. Hulpus et al. (2013) proposed an approach by linking the topics inherent to a text with the concepts in DBpedia[2] and thereby automatically extracting the topic labels from the corpus. Meij et al. (2012) extracted underlying concepts of a text from a large knowledge base of Wikipedia articles by applying a supervised learning using a Naive Bayes (NB), Support Vector Machines (SVM), and a C4.5 decision tree classifier. Large knowledge bases, such as YAGO[3], are also used (Hoffart et al., 2013) to explore the inherent relationship between entities and disambiguate them to derive the context. Taking insights from various research works briefed above, we aim to construct a framework that is inspired by ideas from different works in the next section.

3 The Event Detection & Contextualisation Framework

There are various approaches to extract the information from data, by means of clustering, entity extraction and contextualisation, yet there is no observed pipeline that incorporates different methods and brings them under one framework so as to to generate insights from streaming social media data.

[1] http://nlp.stanford.edu/software/corenlp.shtml
[2] http://dbpedia.org/About
[3] http://www.mpi-inf.mpg.de/departments/databases-and-information-systems/research/yago-naga/yago/

We aim to address this gap, by proposing a framework that performs the aforementioned functionalities under one system. A complete illustration of the framework is visualised in the Figure 1 (further explained in detail). It is a pipeline that incorporates several components, each followed by another phase that uses the output from the previous one. The data could potentially come from various social media APIs; however we have focused on data collected from Twitter streaming API[4]. Following sections explain the different phases, in order, that process the input streaming data: *indexing and clustering*, *entity recognition*, and *entity disambiguation and contextualisation*.

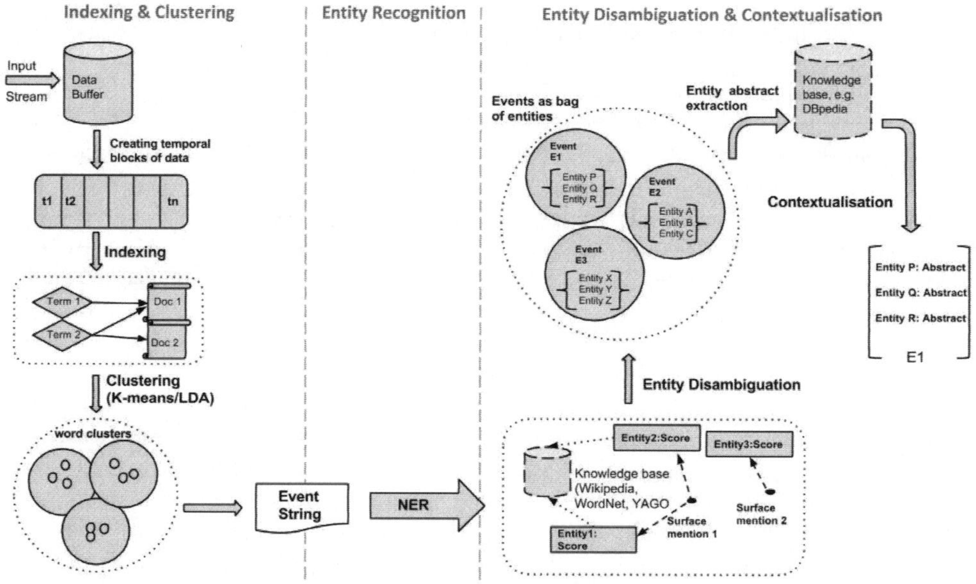

Figure 1. Event detection and Contextualisation framework

3.1 Indexing and Clustering

This phase is aimed at pre-processing the data, breaking the data into set of keywords and generating an index that maps words against their corresponding document. Once an index is created, the data is clustered as sets of word vectors occurring together prominently. These clusters tend to represent the events that exist in the data.

Indexing: The data is indexed in this sub-phase. The incoming data stream is stored and then the divided in slabs of time windows (say of 10 minutes each). This is done to analyse the data based on regular time intervals, which may result in inferring only the highly dominating events/clusters present in the data. An index, between terms and corresponding documents (that initially contained those terms), is generated for this slab of data using standard libraries such as Lucene[5] and Solr[6] (built over Lucene).

Clustering: In this sub-phase we derive the preliminary clusters of the data, which are likely to reflect the most related content within the data slab that was earlier created. Examples of the clustering algorithms that can be hired to cluster the data are k-means, PLSA (Hofmann, 1999) and LDA (Blei et al., 2003). After the clusters are formed, the terms with high weight in the clusters are taken to query the index for retrieving the most relevant documents based threshold relevance score. The relevance score is derived from term frequency and inverse document frequency (*tf-idf*) (Manning et al., 2008) value and accordingly the documents are retrieved. The text from those top scored documents can now be extracted and merged into one string, hereafter called *event string*, which tends to represent the infor-

[4] https://dev.twitter.com/docs/api/streaming
[5] http://lucene.apache.org/
[6] http://lucene.apache.org/solr/

mation stored against a particular cluster or event. This *event string* is further used for NER and disambiguation.

3.2 Entity Recognition

The *event string,* derived above, is further annotated for its entities by applying Named Entity Recognition techniques. NER is an information extraction task to extract key elements, hereafter referred to as *Entities,* from a text and categorise them into person, location, organisation, etc. In this work we rely on libraries such as Stanford NER (Finkel et al., 2005) or other wrappers to this library, which implement it to extract named entities. However, there are other libraries available for this purpose, for instance, Open NLP[7], Open Calais[8], etc. A detailed explanation of the NER models is given in the research work by Sang and Meulder (2003) and Finkel et al. (2005).

For each mention in the string there can be multiple candidate entities which further need to be disambiguated. An explanation of it could be given with an example, such as in "David was playing for Manchester United when Victoria gave her auditions. Victoria later became part of band Spice Girls": how could it be determined whether Victoria is a person (particularly Victoria Beckham) and not Victoria- a place or Queen Victoria, and David implies David Beckham and not David - a figure in religious text/history. Establishing such a mapping between mention and most relevant entity is termed as named entity disambiguation process.

3.3 Entity Disambiguation and Contextualisation

In the entity disambiguation and contextualisation phase, initially an input text (web page, language paragraph, sentence, article) is resolved into various mentions of entities (surface mentions- that means its just a mention with no associated knowledge) by matching all the potential candidate entities with the surface mentions. For this purpose Stanford NER tagger is used. For each mention (a potential entity) knowledge sources such as DBpedia and/or Yago (Hoffart et al., 2013; Hoffart et al., 2011) are harvested to extract potential entity mentions. Each mention will then be mapped for numerous potential entity candidates. After extracting the candidate entities, a relevance score can be assigned to each based on features such as *a prior for candidate entity popularity*, *mutual information* (similarity between key-phrase or query string and description of the entity), *syntax based similarity* (Thater et al., 2010), *entity-entity coherence* (quantifying the number of similar incoming links on a knowledge base as Wikipedia). Milne and Witten (2008) extended few similarity measures defined by Bunescu and Pasca (2006), which compared the context of a given text to the entities mention in Wikipedia.

Considering the above features, a graph of mentions and candidate entities, with the edges as weights, can be generated. Each node will have a certain weight on its edge, a greedy approach can be adopted to iteratively remove the low weight nodes to disambiguate the entities (Hoffart et al., 2011). This approach will result in disambiguated entities (to a high degree) for each surface mentions of the input text and represent entities according to the context of the input text. After the disambiguation of the entities, a knowledge resource can be hired to query for generating a brief description about the prominent entities (such as their *abstract/description* and *type*), and thereby contextualising the whole input text with a bag of entities and their corresponding description.

The overall framework describes a mechanism to design a tool that can process input streaming data into set of clusters that reflect events and assists in visualising the context of those events. This framework is considered to enhance event detection approaches by enriching the events with their relevant information being extracted from knowledge resources. While some of the state of the art techniques and tools incorporated in this framework have been proposed and/or utilised in other domains, the proposed framework is a novel end-to-end pipeline specifically designed for the news industry and for breaking event detection and contextualisation.

4 Conclusion and Future Work

This paper presents a framework, which aims at assisting journalists in dealing with the ever- flooding UGC to detect the upcoming/breaking events. Various surveys (Oriella, 2013; Cision, 2013; Heravi et.

[7] https://opennlp.apache.org/
[8] http://www.opencalais.com/

al., 2014) highlight the growing need for specialised tools to allow journalists utilise the user-generated for news production and storytelling. The proposed framework is believed to be an important step forward in addressing the challenges encountered by journalists in leveraging the social media content for emerging event detection and event contextualisation in the process of news production. The emerging events can now be visualised without needing to manually assess the frequency of any particular information propagation on social media and also generate the context of the information at the same time.

An early phase test was performed on the proposed pipeline so as to assess the viability of the framework. The framework was simulated with a sample data constituting of tweets from three different known events and it reflected encouraging results with respect to the viability of the underlying processes and the framework as a whole. The framework successfully clustered the sample data, using *k-means* algorithm, into unique clusters and the entity disambiguation phase, implemented using AIDA framework (Hoffart et al., 2011), yielded relevant entities. An end-to-end evaluation of the pipeline, however, is yet to be performed to analyse the results of every phase, and the pipeline as a whole.

There are foreseen challenges such as noise filtering, the non-lexical nature of the data, and the verity of the content. The data from social media contains an enormous amount of noise (such as random tweets posted by users which do not have a relevance with the event and may yet contain the filtering keywords) in exhaustive social media streams when it comes to filtering the content specific to certain events/topics and that could certainly affect the outcome of the event clusters. Apart from noise, often the language used on social media is non-lexical and non-syntactic in nature because users compromise with the language rules to share more information in limited space (e.g. Twitter allows only 140 characters) hence leveraging the NLP techniques may not result in most efficient results.

The above challenges require a thorough investigation of the current state of the research and as a future work we aim to address 1) perform an end-to-end evaluation on the pipeline and 2) address the above challenges by exploring how information extraction techniques can be customised for syntactically and lexically inefficient data and thereby refine the information gathering processes for journalists.

Acknowledgement

This publication has emanated from research conducted with the financial support of Science Foundation Ireland (SFI) under Grant Numbers 12/TIDA/I2389, SFI/12/RC/2289 and 13/TIDA/I2743.

References

Allan, J. 2002. Introduction to topic detection and tracking. In Topic detection and tracking (pp. 1-16). Springer US.

Blei, D. M., Ng, A. Y., & Jordan, M. I. 2003. Latent dirichlet allocation. the Journal of machine Learning research, 3, 993-1022.

Bunescu, R. C., & Pasca, M. 2006. Using Encyclopedic Knowledge for Named entity Disambiguation. In EACL (Vol. 6, pp. 9-16).

Cision. 2013. Social Journalism Study 2013. Report by Cision & Canterbury Christ Church University (UK). http://www.cision.com/uk/wp-content/uploads/2014/05/Social-Journalism-Study-2013.pdf visited July 13th,2014

Finkel, J. R., Grenager, T., & Manning, C. 2005, June. Incorporating non-local information into information extraction systems by gibbs sampling. In Proceedings of the 43rd Annual Meeting on Association for Computational Linguistics (pp. 363-370). Association for Computational Linguistics.

Heravi, B. R., Boran, M., & Breslin, J. 2012. Towards Social Semantic Journalism. In Sixth International AAAI Conference on Weblogs and Social Media.

Heravi, B. R., & McGinnis, J. 2013. A Framework for Social Semantic Journalism. In First International IFIP Working Conference on Value-Driven Social & Semantic Collective Intelligence (VaSCo), at ACM Web Science.

Heravi, B. R., Harrower, N., Boran, M. 2014. Social Journalism Survey: First National Study on Irish Journalists' use of Social Media. HuJo, Insight Centre for Data Analytics, National University of Ireland, Galway (forthcoming 20 July 2014).

Hoffart, J., Yosef, M. A., Bordino, I., Fürstenau, H., Pinkal, M., Spaniol, M., Taneva, B., Thater, S., Weikum, G. 2011. Robust disambiguation of named entities in text. InProceedings of the Conference on Empirical Methods in Natural Language Processing (pp. 782-792). Association for Computational Linguistics.

Hofmann, T. 1999. Probabilistic latent semantic analysis. InProceedings of the Fifteenth conference on Uncertainty in artificial intelligence(pp. 289-296). Morgan Kaufmann Publishers Inc.

Hoffart, J., Suchanek, F. M., Berberich, K., & Weikum, G. 2013. YAGO2: A spatially and temporally enhanced knowledge base from Wikipedia. Artificial Intelligence, 194, 28-61.

Hulpus, I., Hayes, C., Karnstedt, M., & Greene, D. 2013. Unsupervised graph-based topic labelling using DBpedia. In Proceedings of the sixth ACM international conference on Web search and data mining (pp. 465-474). ACM.

Manning, C. D., Raghavan, P., & Schütze, H. 2008. Introduction to information retrieval (Vol. 1, p. 6). Cambridge: Cambridge university press.

Meij, E., Weerkamp, W., & de Rijke, M. 2012. Adding semantics to microblog posts. In Proceedings of the fifth ACM international conference on Web search and data mining (pp. 563-572). ACM.

Milne, D., & Witten, I. H. 2008. Learning to link with wikipedia. In Proceedings of the 17th ACM conference on Information and knowledge management (pp. 509-518). ACM.

Muthukrishnan, S. 2005. Data streams: Algorithms and applications. Now Publishers Inc.

Oriella. 2013. The New Normal for News: Have global media Changed forever Oriella PR Network Global Digital Journalism Study 2013. Available from http://www.oriellaprnetwork.com/sites/default/files/research/Brands2Life_ODJS_v4.pdf visited July 13th,2014

Osborne, M., Petrovic, S., McCreadie, R., Macdonald, C., & Ounis, I. 2012. Bieber no more: First story detection using Twitter and Wikipedia. InProceedings of the Workshop on Time-aware Information Access. TAIA (Vol. 12).

Parikh, R., & Karlapalem, K. 2013. Et: events from tweets. InProceedings of the 22nd international conference on World Wide Web companion (pp. 613-620). International World Wide Web Conferences Steering Committee.

Petrović, S., Osborne, M., & Lavrenko, V. 2010. Streaming first story detection with application to twitter. In Human Language Technologies: The 2010 Annual Conference of the North American Chapter of the Association for Computational Linguistics (pp. 181-189). Association for Computational Linguistics.

Ritter, A., Clark, S., & Etzioni, O. 2011. Named entity recognition in tweets: an experimental study. In Proceedings of the Conference on Empirical Methods in Natural Language Processing (pp. 1524-1534). Association for Computational Linguistics.

Ritter, A., Etzioni, O., & Clark, S. 2012. Open domain event extraction from twitter. In Proceedings of the 18th ACM SIGKDD international conference on Knowledge discovery and data mining (pp. 1104-1112). ACM.

Thater, S., Fürstenau, H., & Pinkal, M. 2010. Contextualizing semantic representations using syntactically enriched vector models. In Proceedings of the 48th Annual Meeting of the Association for Computational Linguistics (pp. 948-957). Association for Computational Linguistics.

Tjong Kim Sang, E. F., & De Meulder, F. 2003. Introduction to the CoNLL-2003 shared task: Language independent named entity recognition. InProceedings of the seventh conference on Natural language learning at HLT-NAACL 2003-Volume 4 (pp. 142-147). Association for Computational Linguistics.

Zaki, M. J., & Meira Jr, W. 2011. Fundamentals of data mining algorithms.